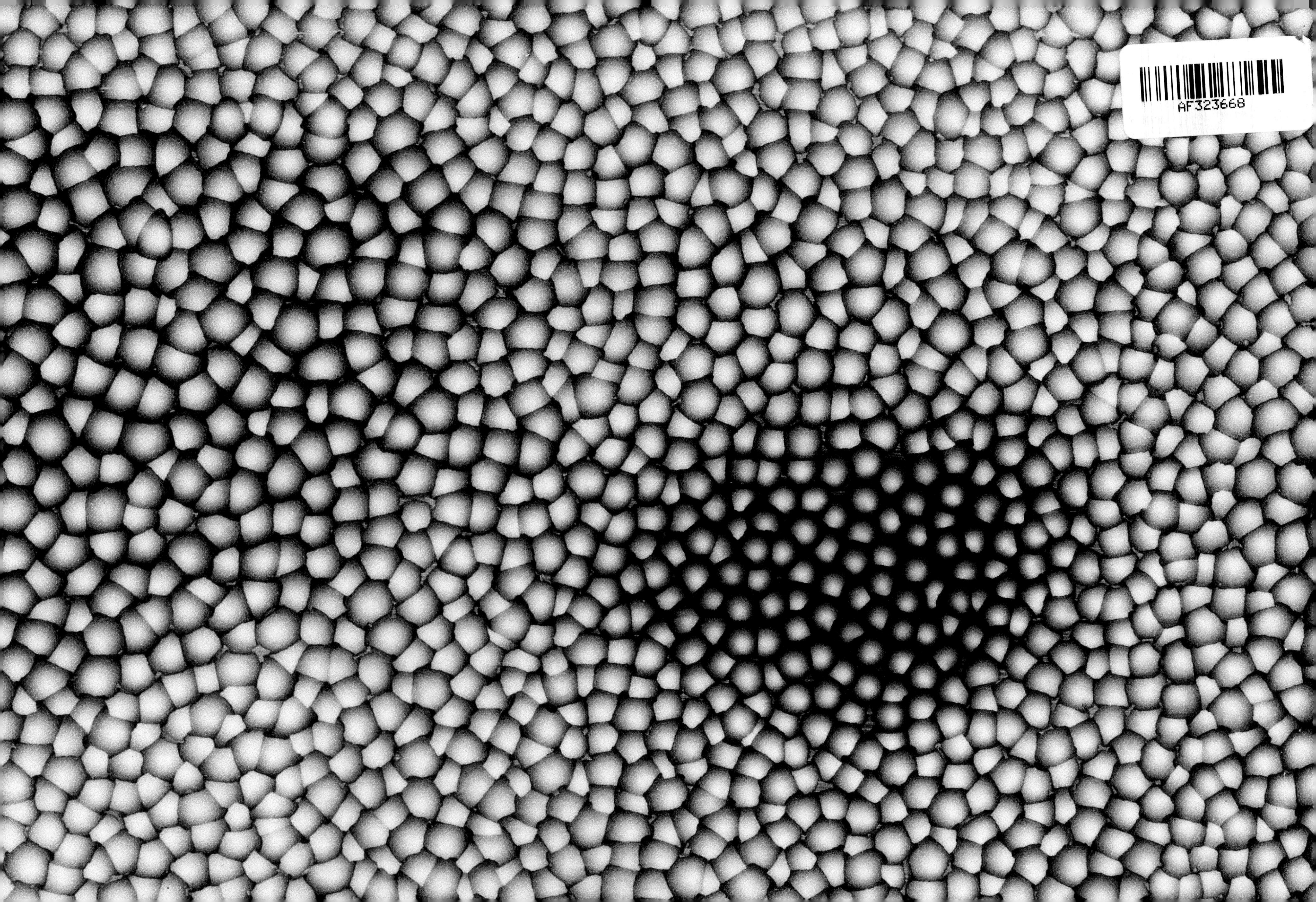
AF323668

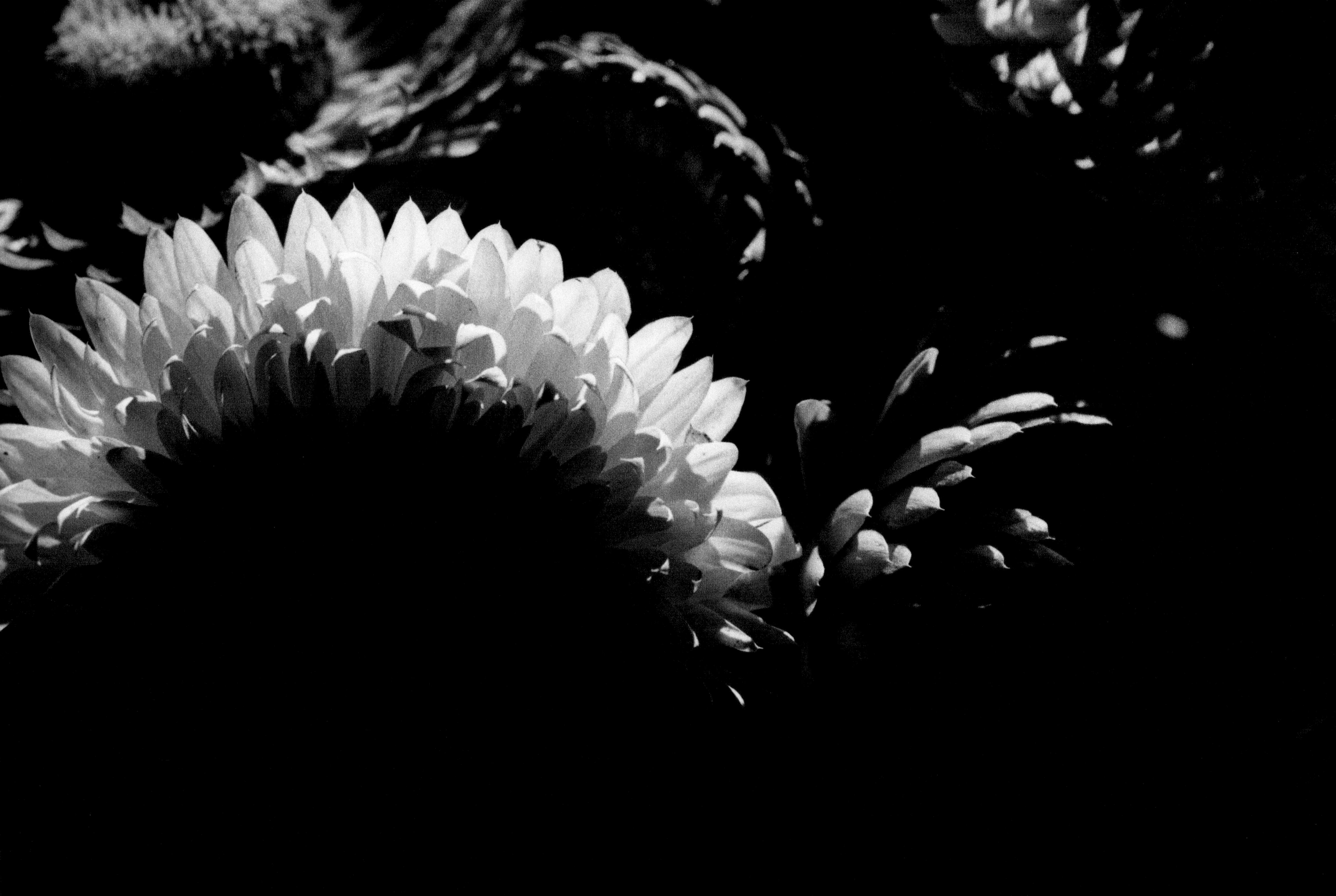

ross bleckner

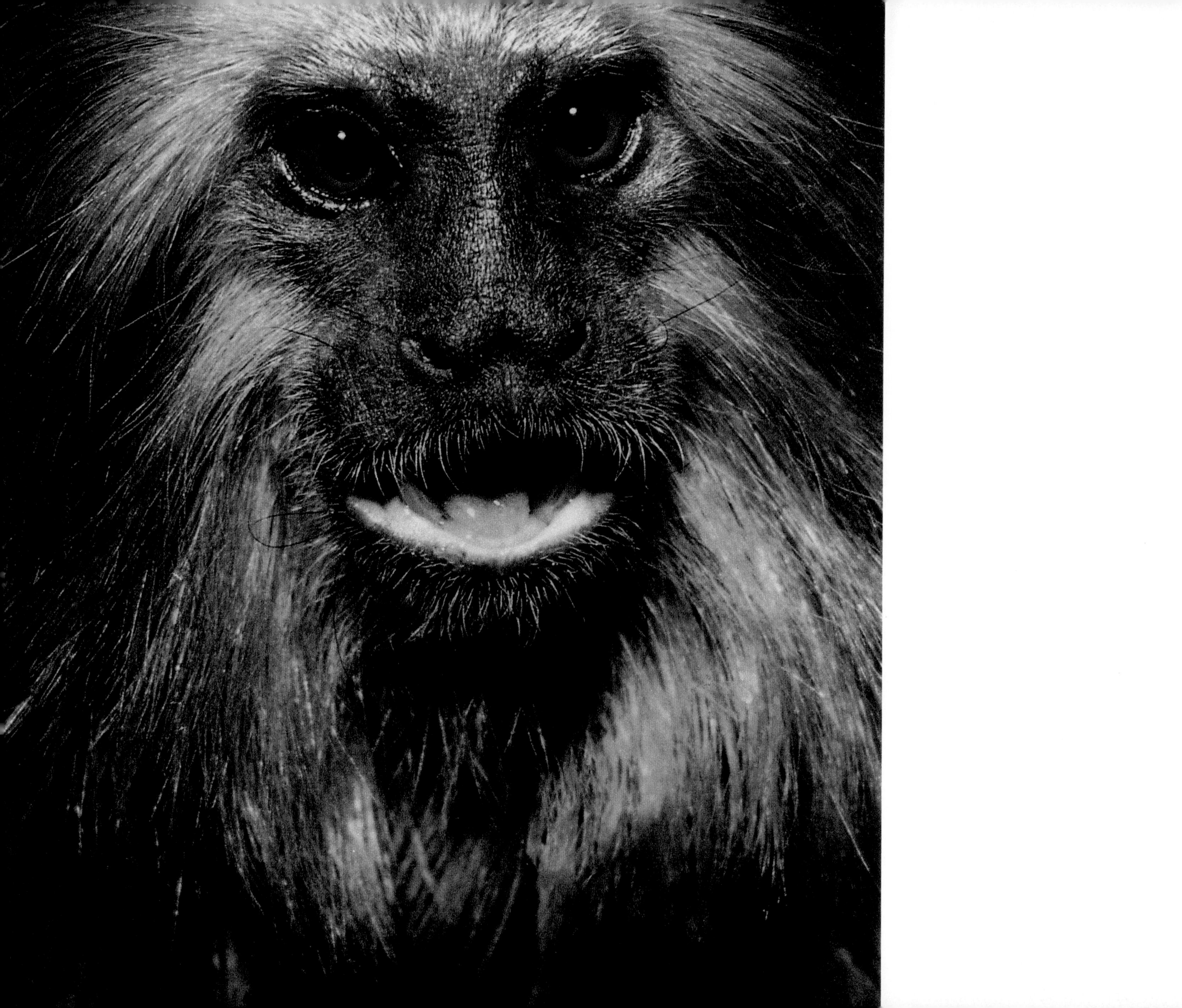

page three

his epigraph:

"He who learns mu[st]
even in our sleep pa[in]
forget falls drop by [...]
heart, and in our despa[ir]
will, comes wisdom
awful grace of God."

st suffer. And
n that cannot
drop upon the
ir, against our
to us by the

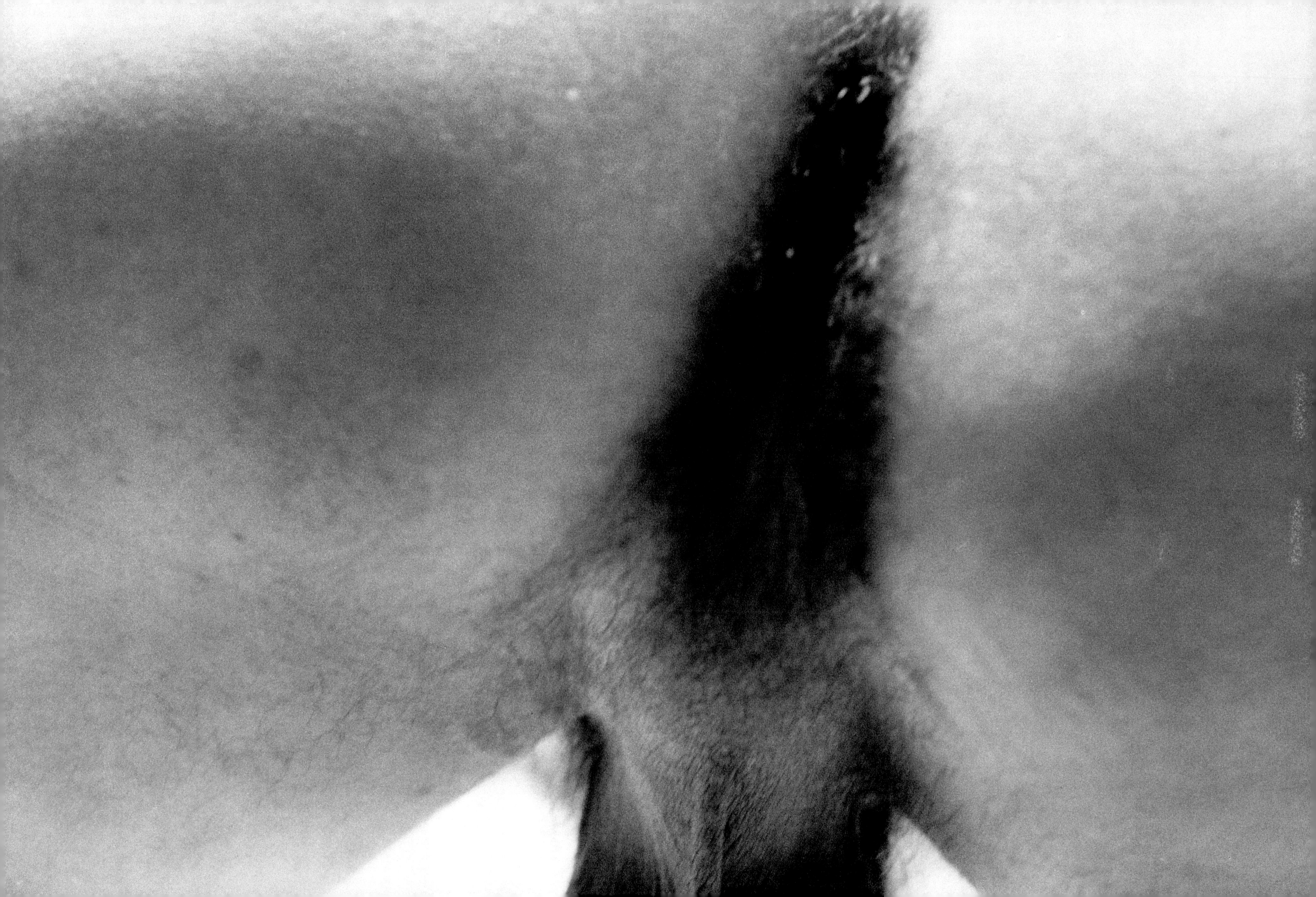

ow
the
we
like
pea
far
roa
mi
ver
noi

are two roads, really: the one
travel down as though life were
that, the dust behind us disap-
ring along with the barns, the
ms, the trees; and that same
d's image in the novel's wayward
ror — convoluted, multiple, in-
ted, simultaneous, continuous,
tless, cracked — that is to say,

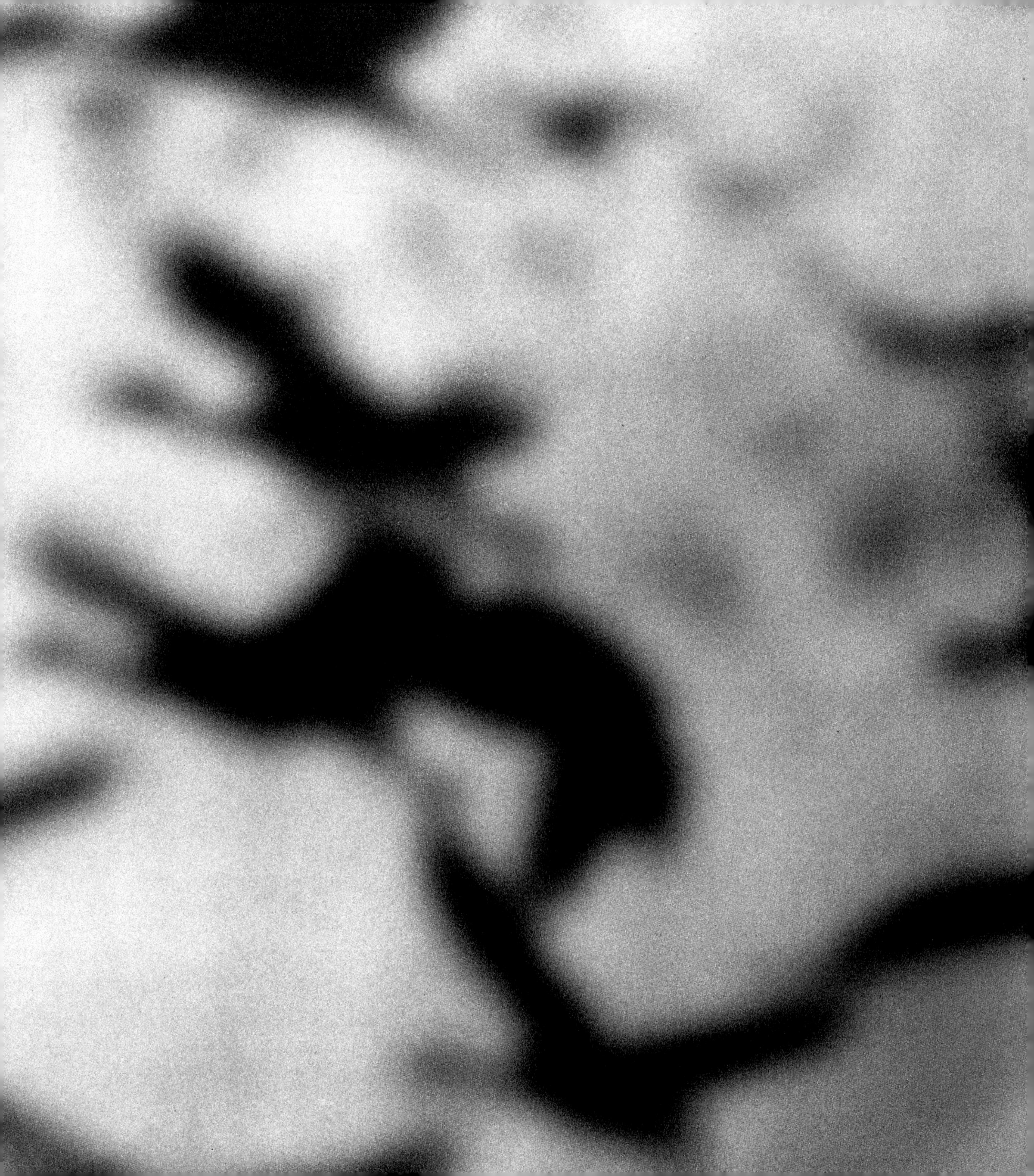

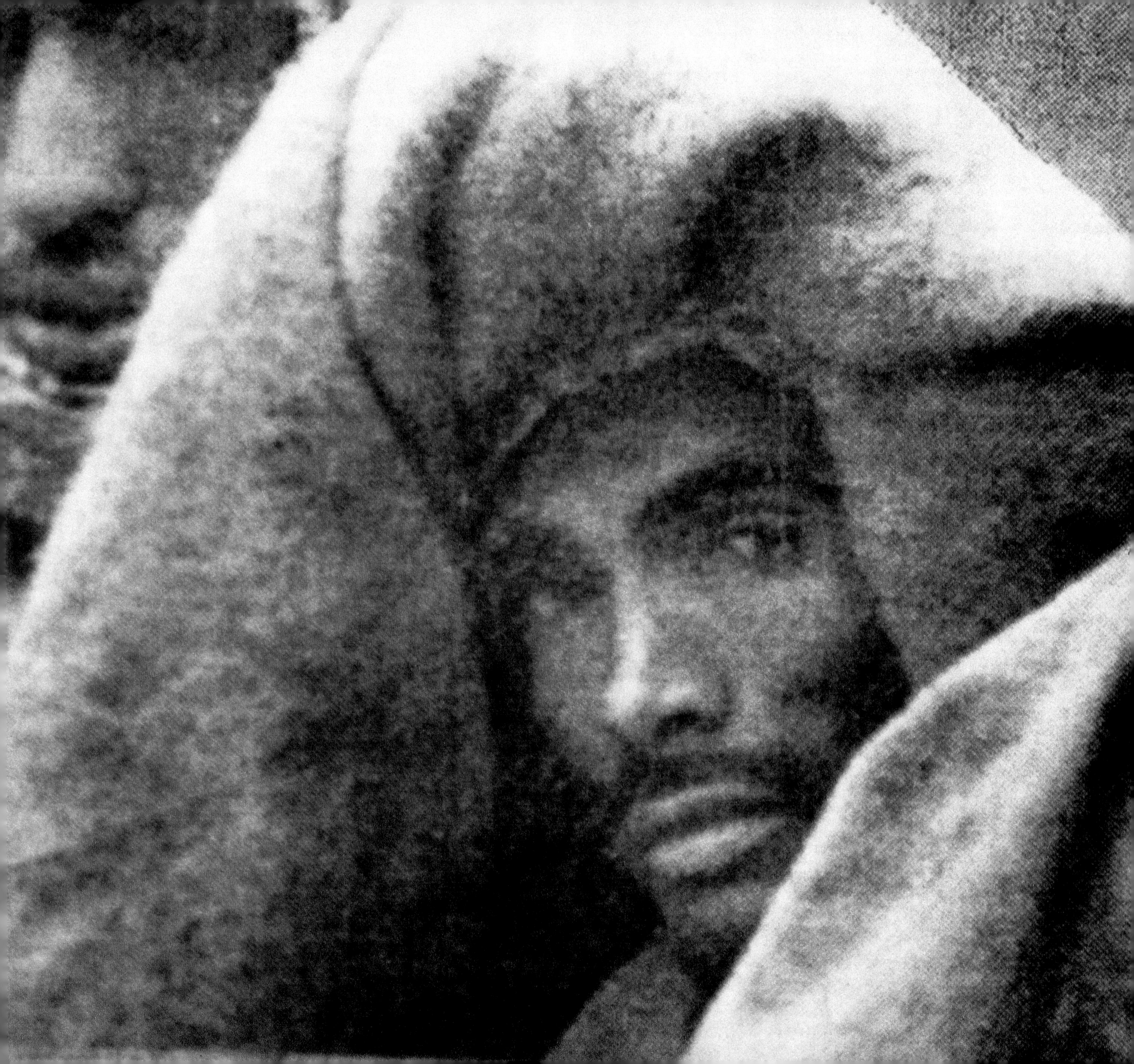

worth. "He did not go in for being an important writer, though he was one; or an important anything. Writing was what mattered to him. The fascination of it. The difficulties. The happiness of getting it down right. The whole area in which artists, in their absorption and single-mindedness, are like solitary children playing with building blocks or crayons or clay."

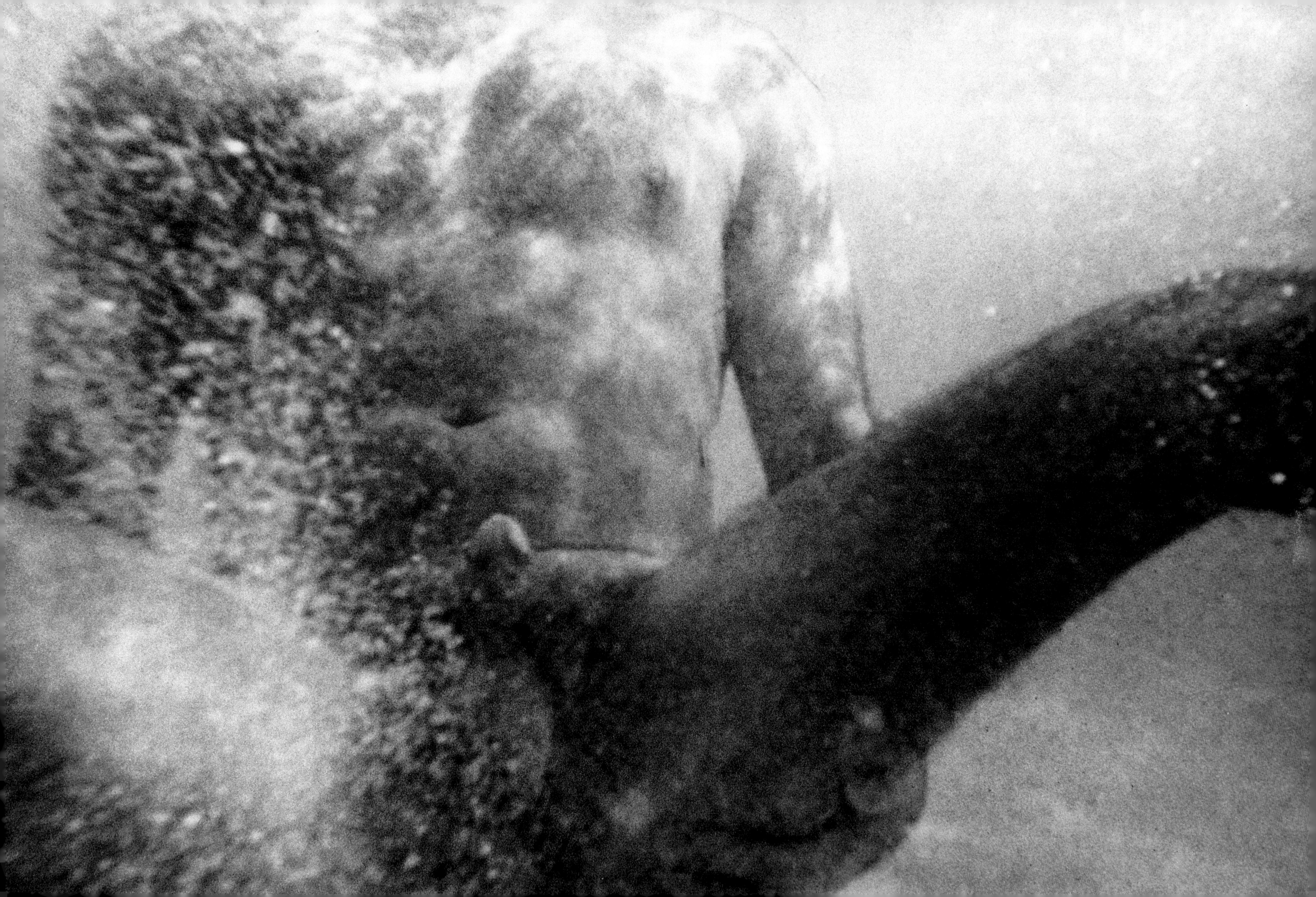

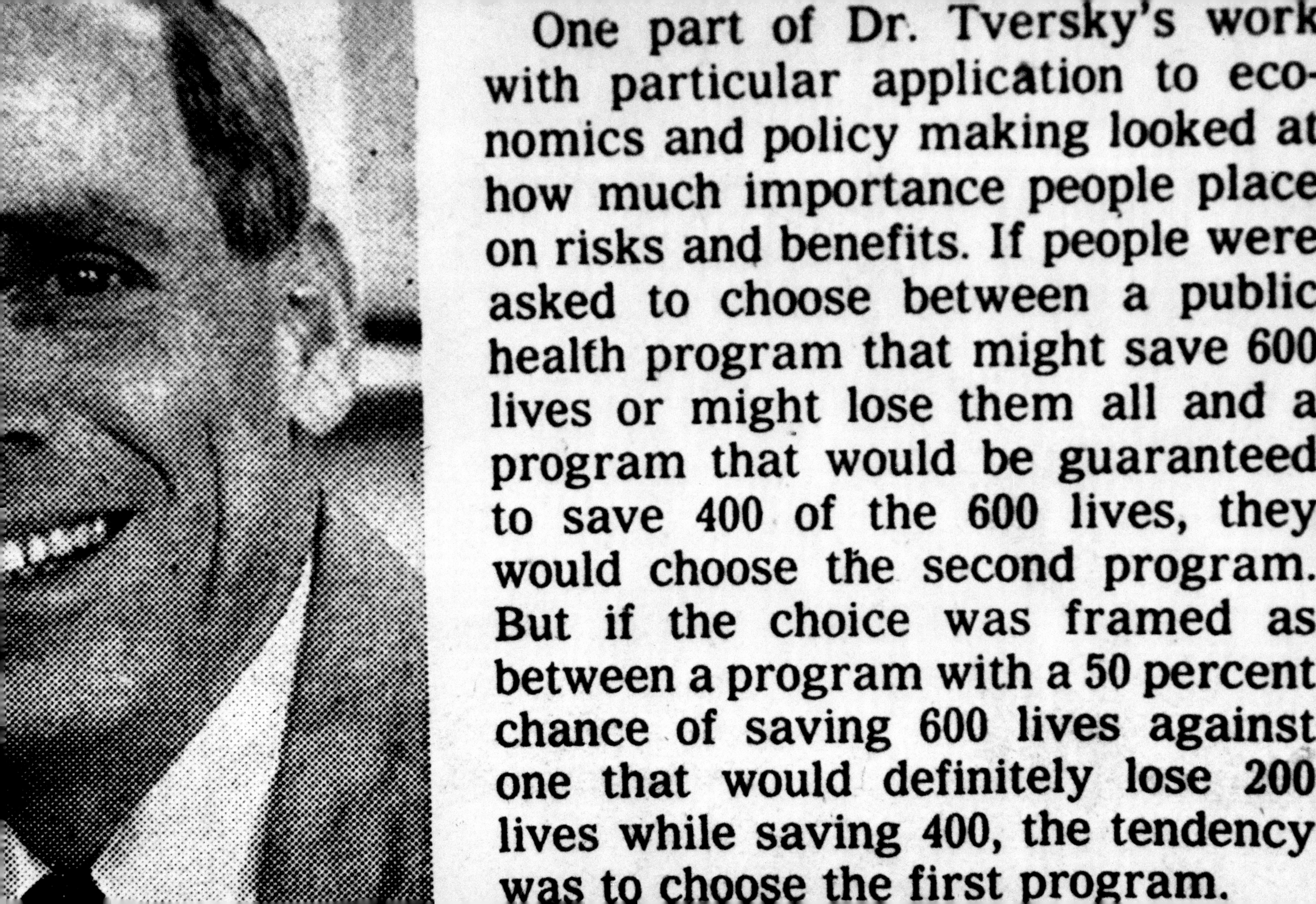

One part of Dr. Tversky's work with particular application to economics and policy making looked at how much importance people place on risks and benefits. If people were asked to choose between a public health program that might save 600 lives or might lose them all and a program that would be guaranteed to save 400 of the 600 lives, they would choose the second program. But if the choice was framed as between a program with a 50 percent chance of saving 600 lives against one that would definitely lose 200 lives while saving 400, the tendency was to choose the first program.

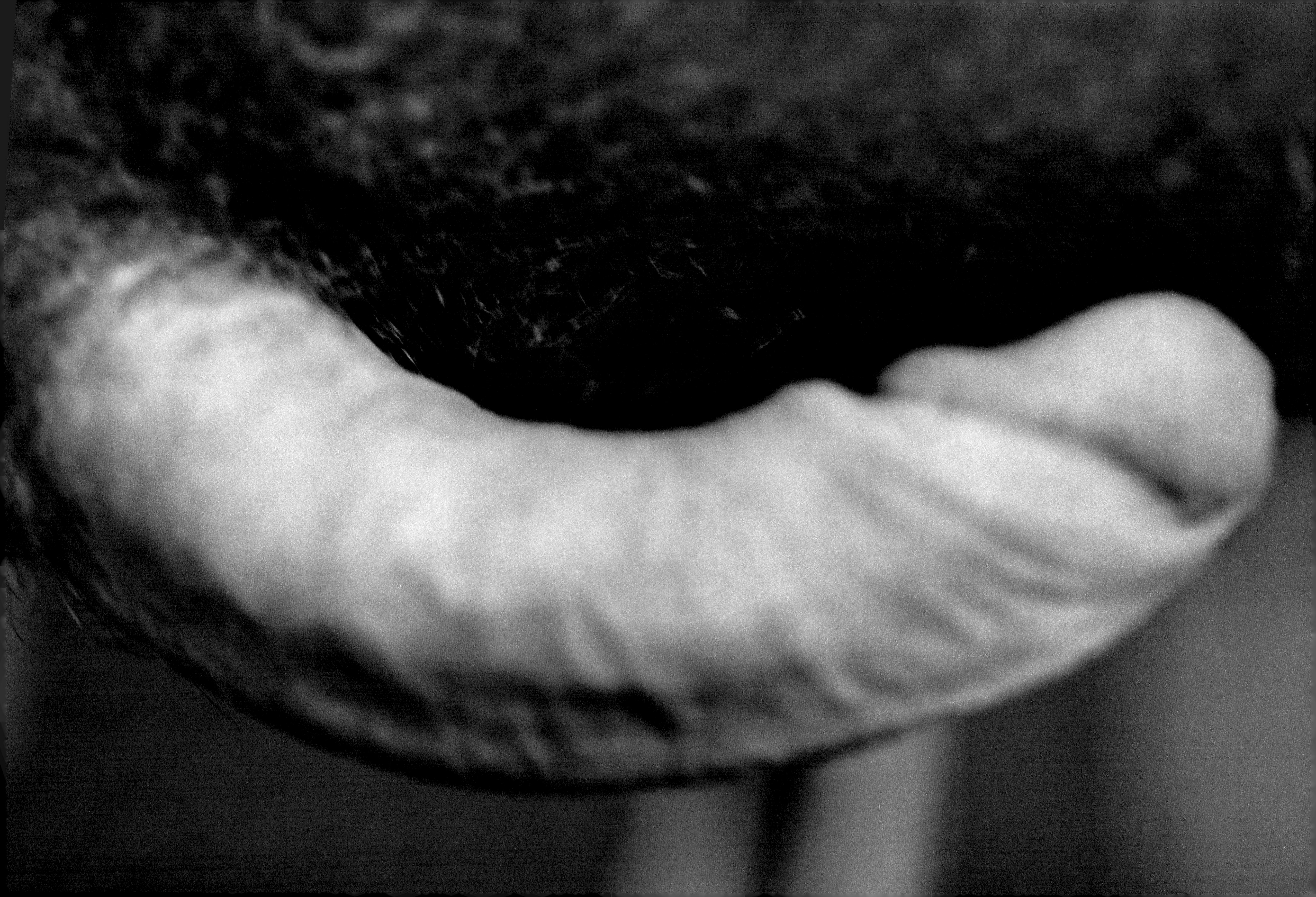

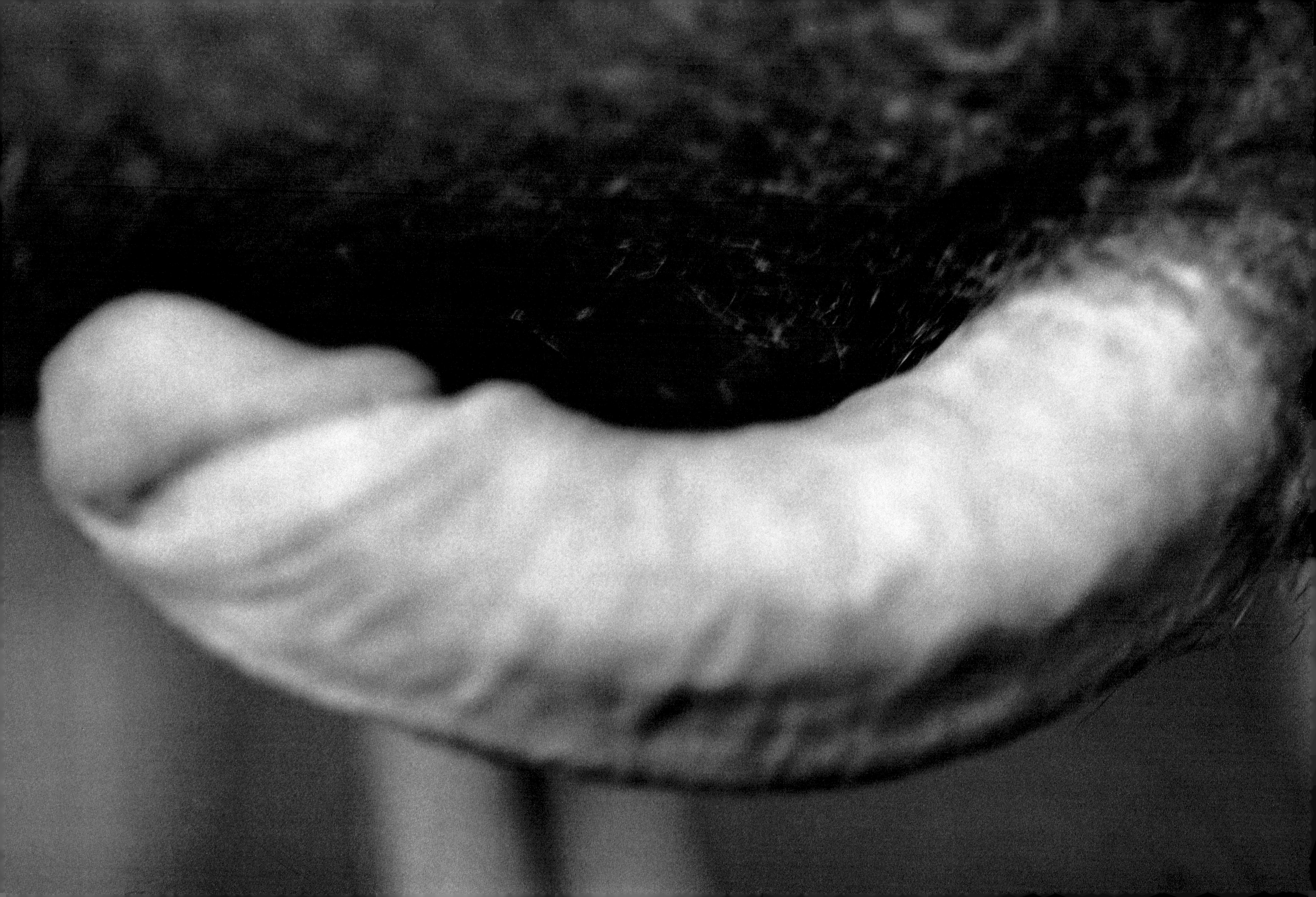

"He was put on earth, it seems, not merely to provide an anodyne to sorrow and an antidote to loss," he writes, "but to trouble our rest, to remind us that all is not well, that neither the center nor the perimeter can hold, that things are not what they seem to be, that masquerade and reality may well be interchangeable, that love is frail, life transient, faith unstable."

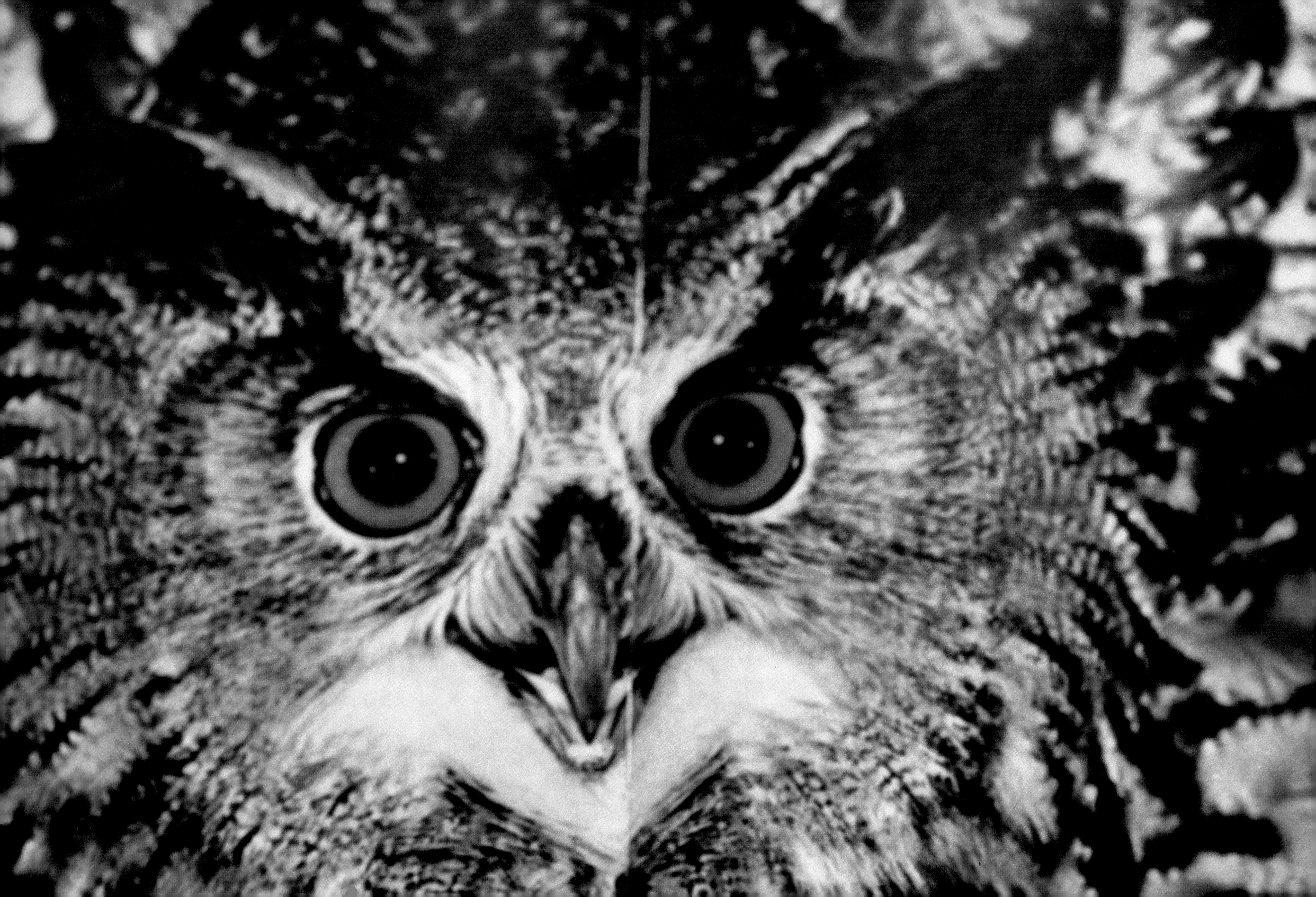

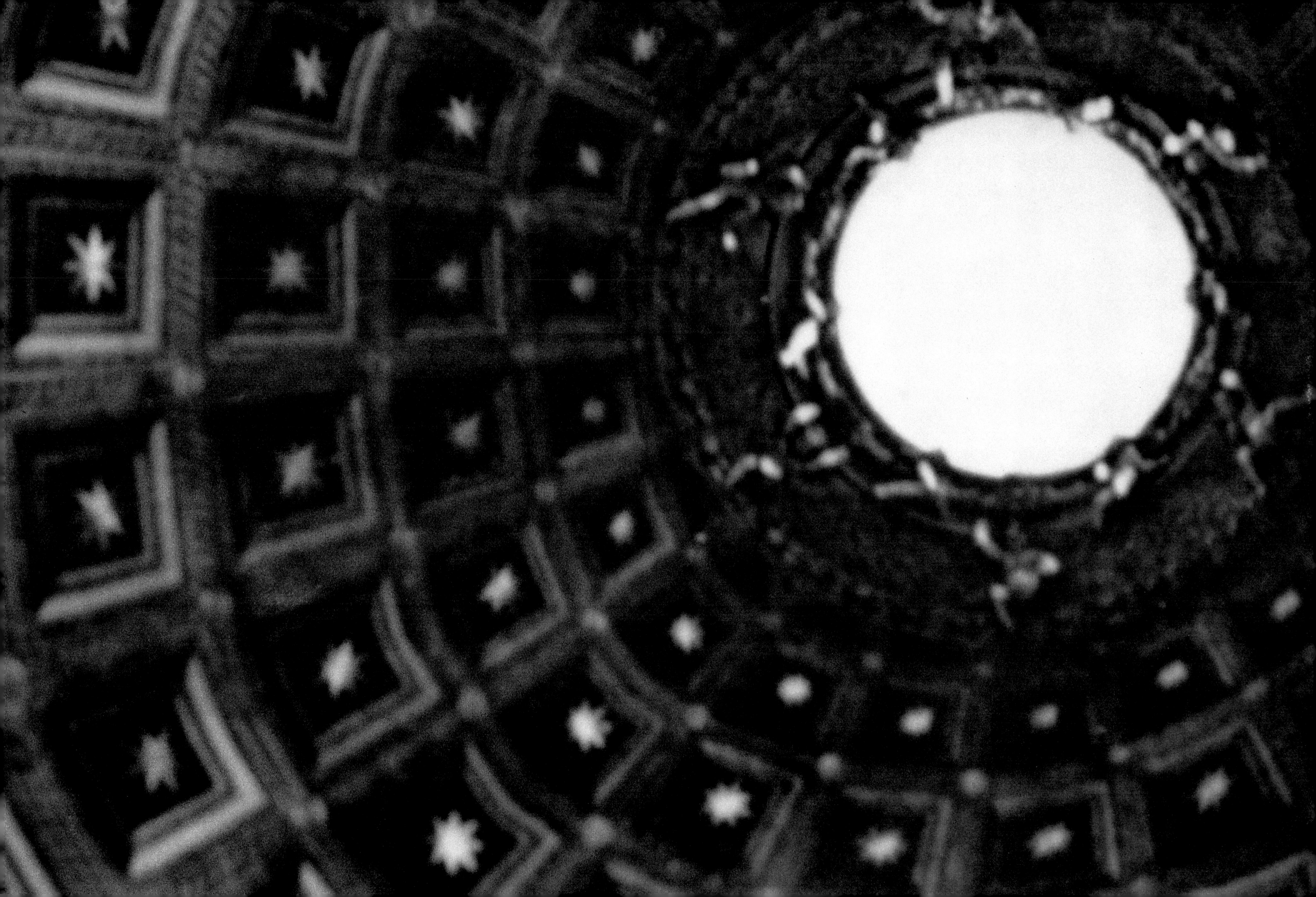

materials of their co
earned that suffering se
ose; that the good guy
hat most explanations o
make the mess I was in
were self-serving lies."

percent fell by more than a fifth, from 19 percent to 15 percent."

The report said, "These trends are mirrored in financial net worth, which is distributed even more unequally than total household wealth. In 1989, the top 1 percent of families as ranked by financial wealth owned 48 percent of the total." The top 20 percent of Americans "accounted for 94 percent of total financial

Treated like objects, they have been insulted, belittled, and betrayed. To resist this tide survivors — and they are becoming ever fewer — have only words, poor, ineffectual words, with which to defend the dead. So some of us weave these words into tales, stories and pleas for memory and decency. It is all we can do, for the living, and for the dead."

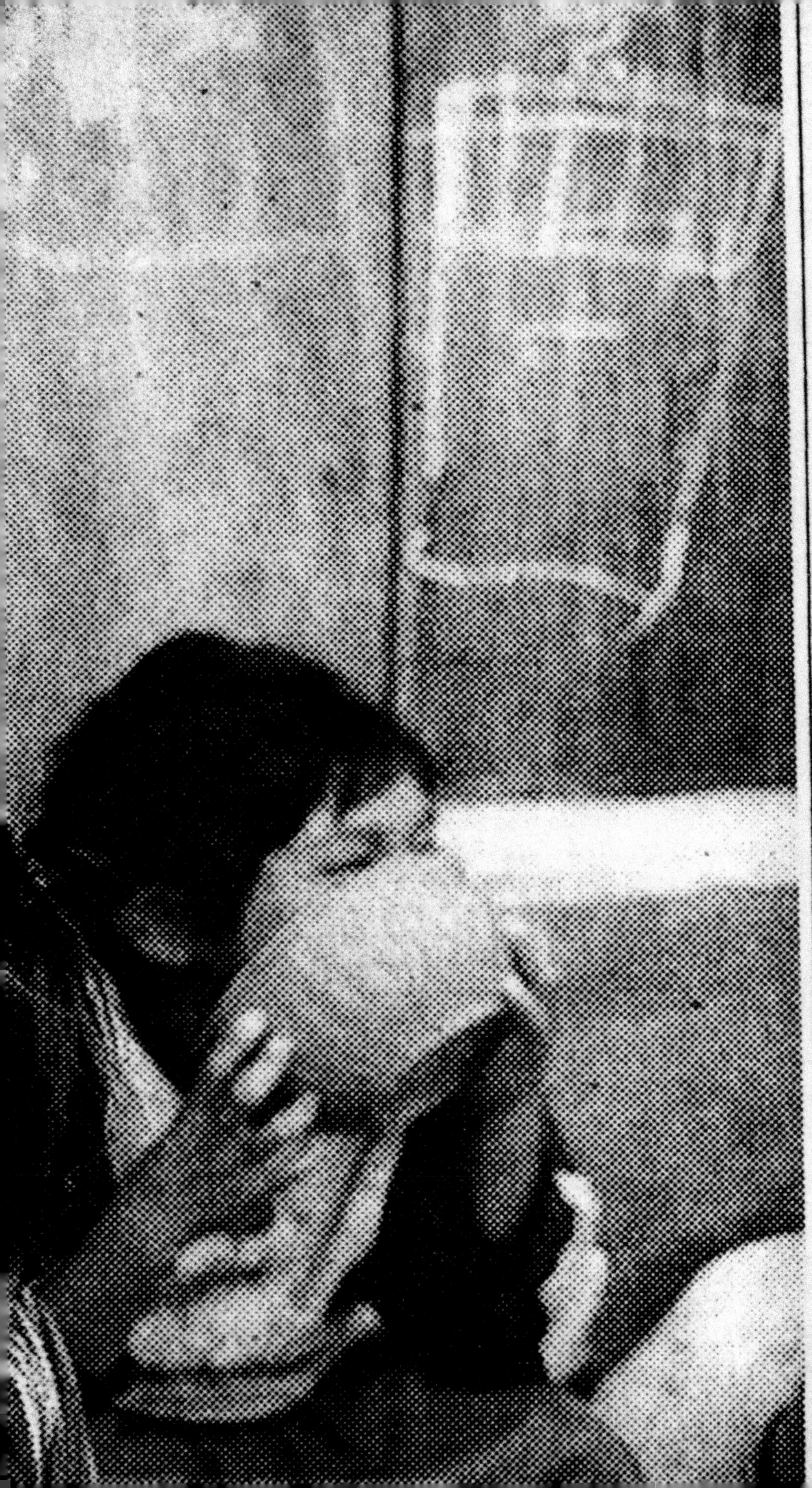

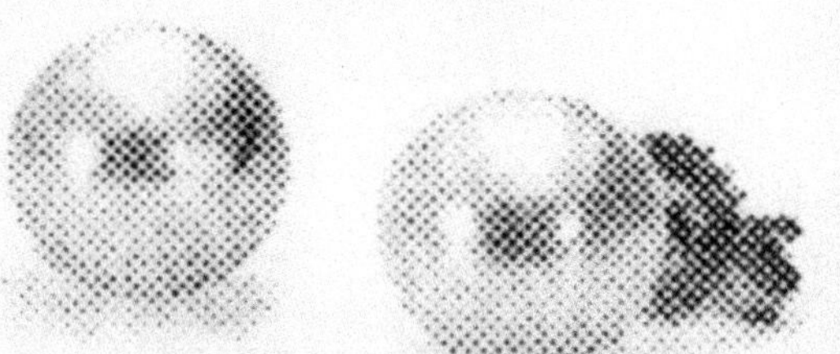

Tiffany Pearls

A woman's jewelry wardrobe starts with the classics—
timeless, understated designs like Tiffany pearl stud earrings.
Cultured pearls of exceptional luster matched for color,
size and shape and set in eighteen karat gold.
Priced from $135 to $2,450.

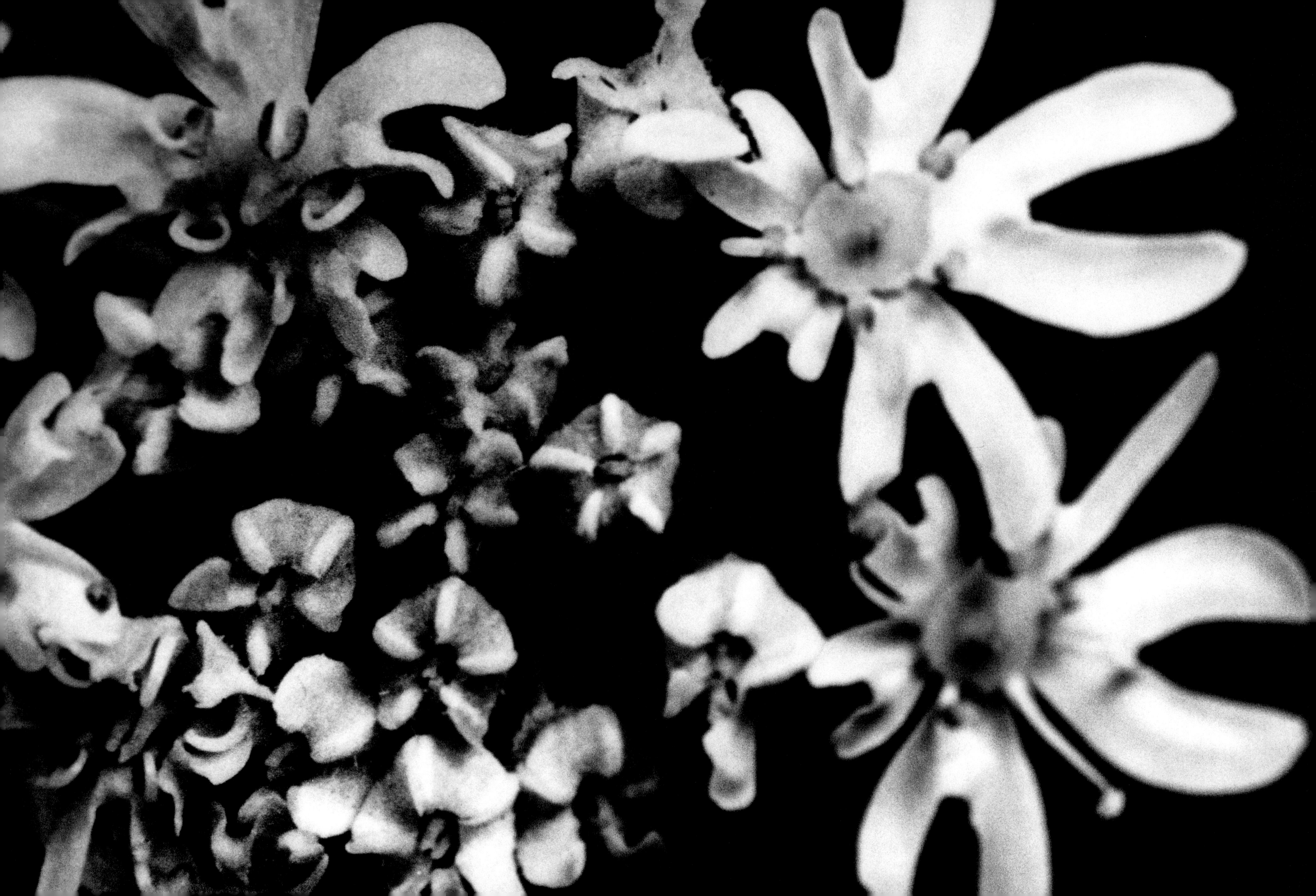

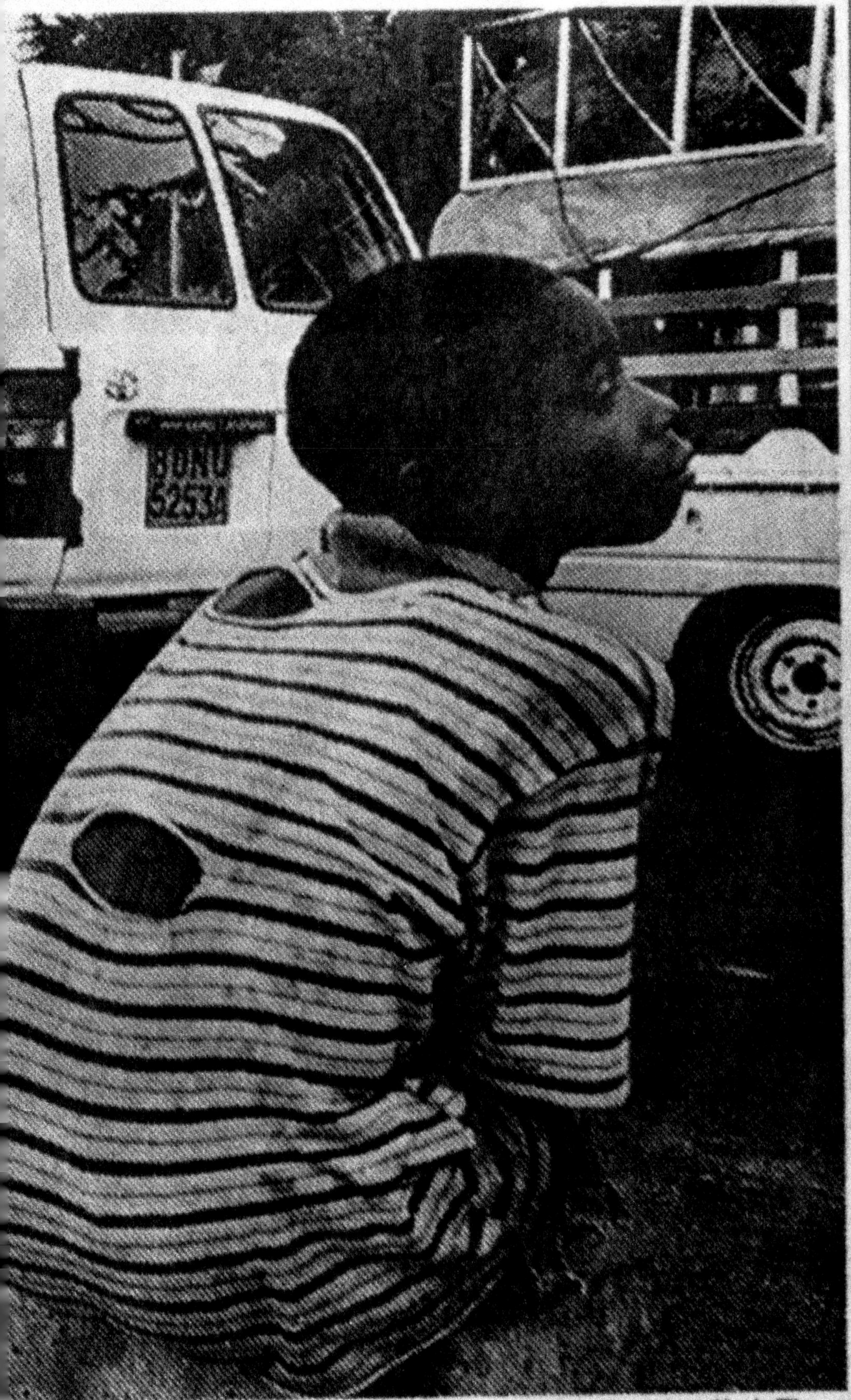

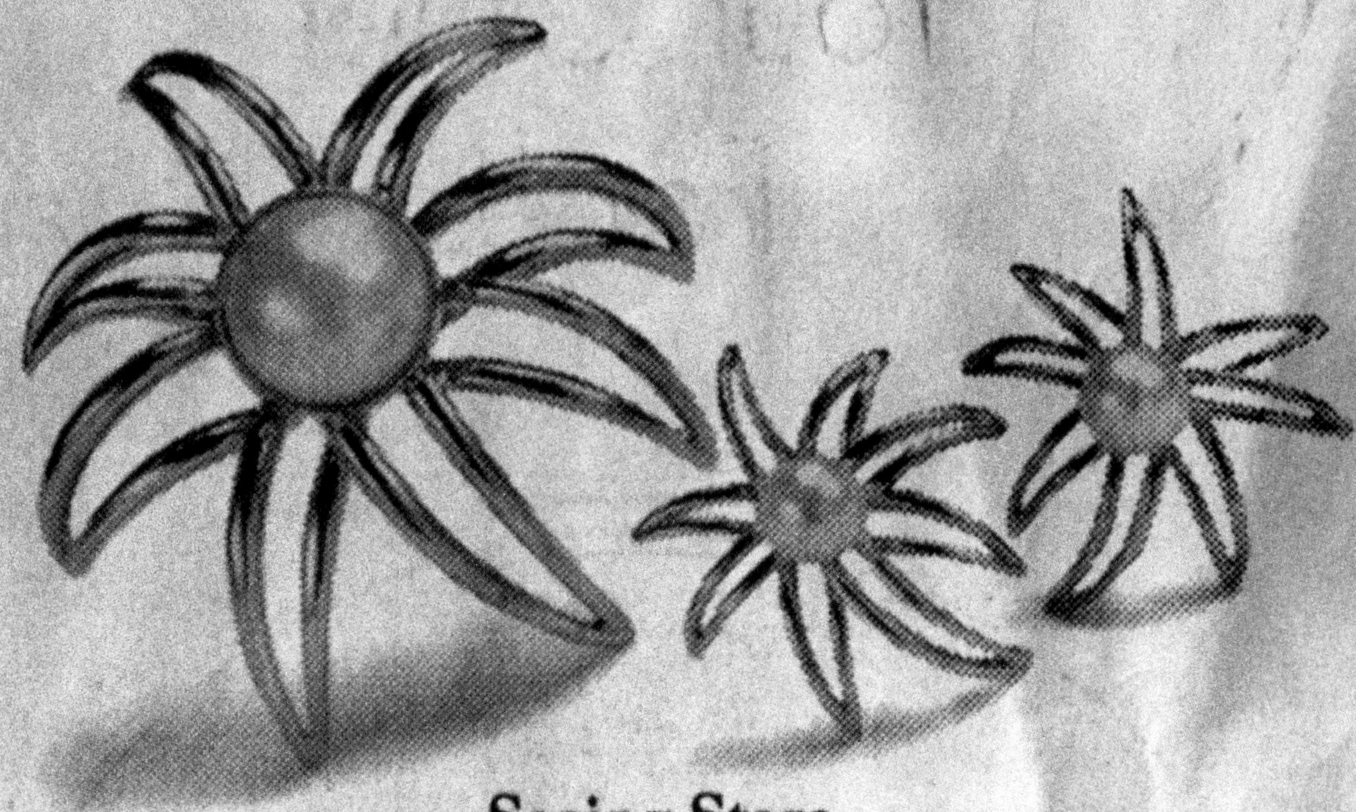

Seeing Stars

Tiffany Fireworks designs in eighteen karat gold.
Brooch with mabe pearl, $2,150.

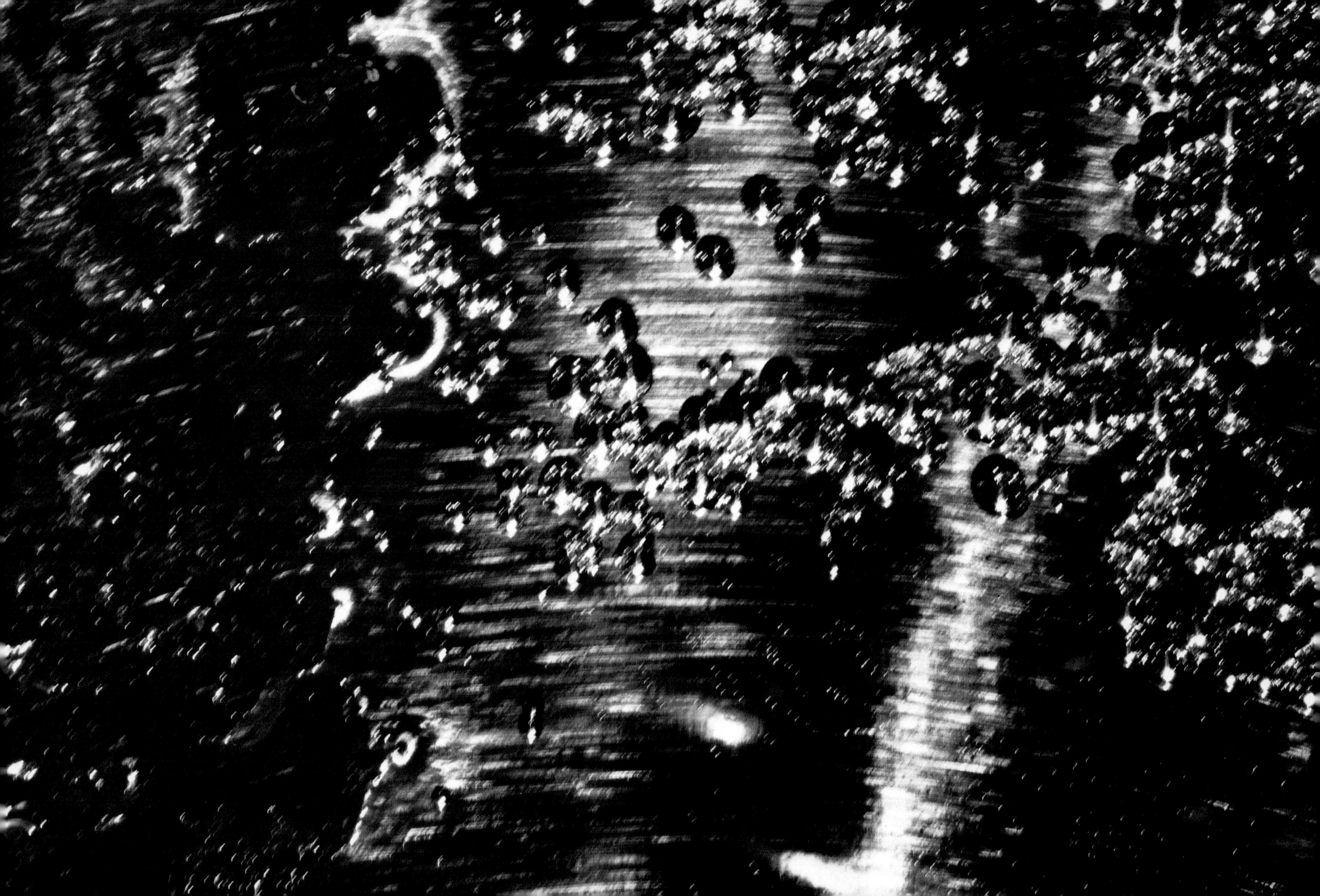

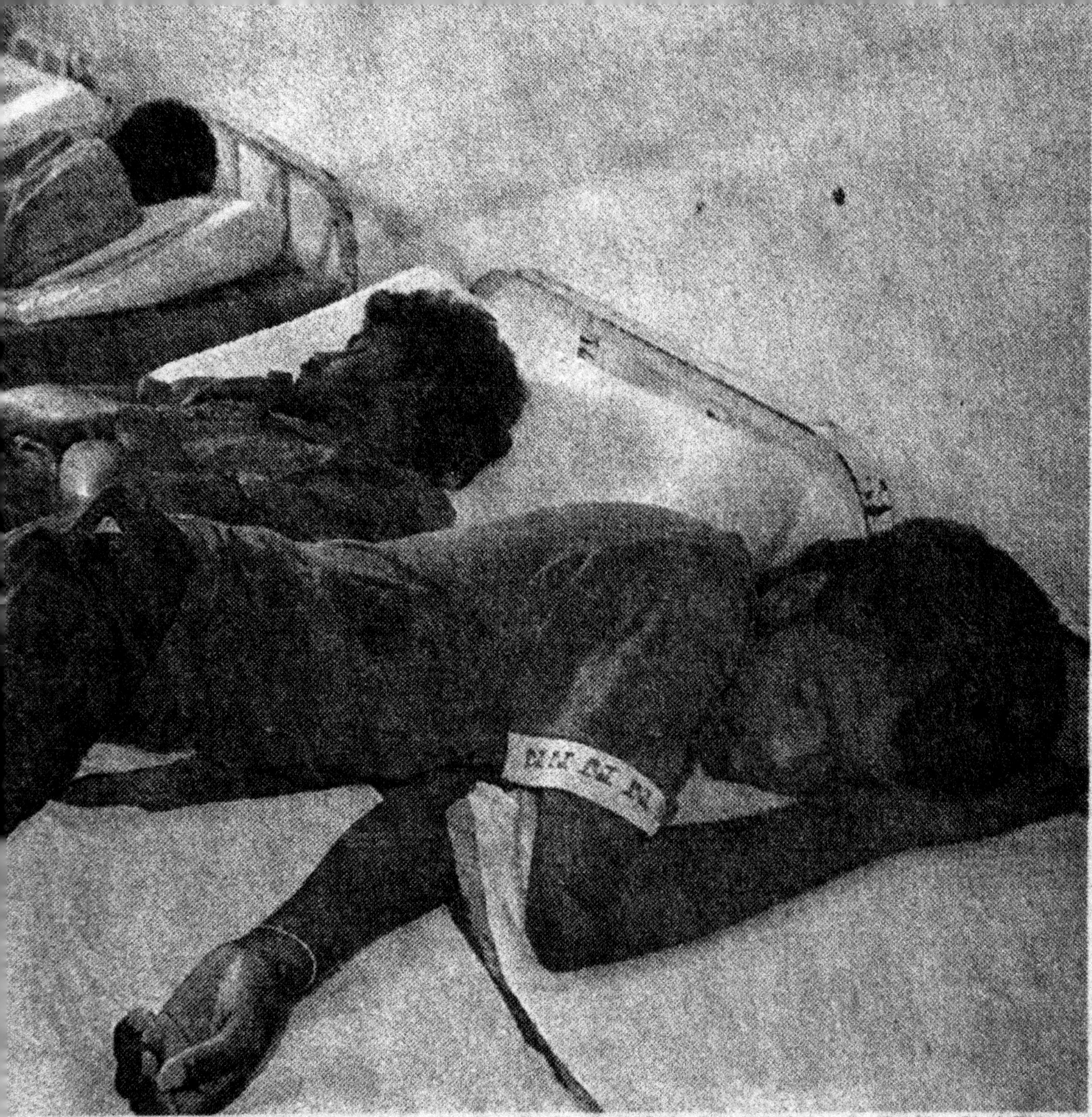

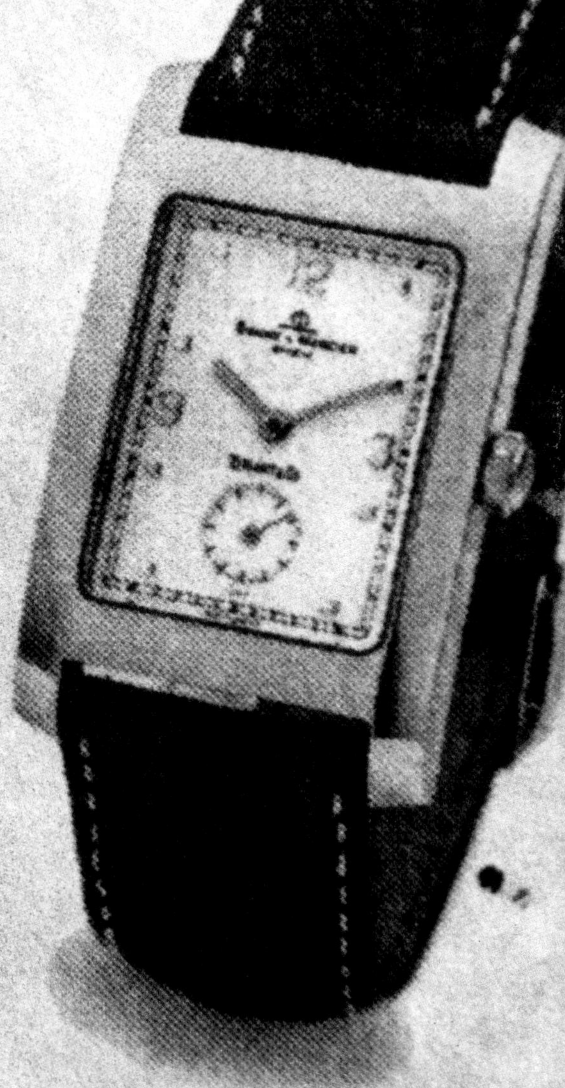

Photographs by Laszlo Beliczay for The New York Times

had punched a hole to get air. Eighteen of their countrymen and one
woman died when the truck driver abandoned them 20 miles from the
Austrian border and fled, leaving a second container padlocked.

Time of Your Life

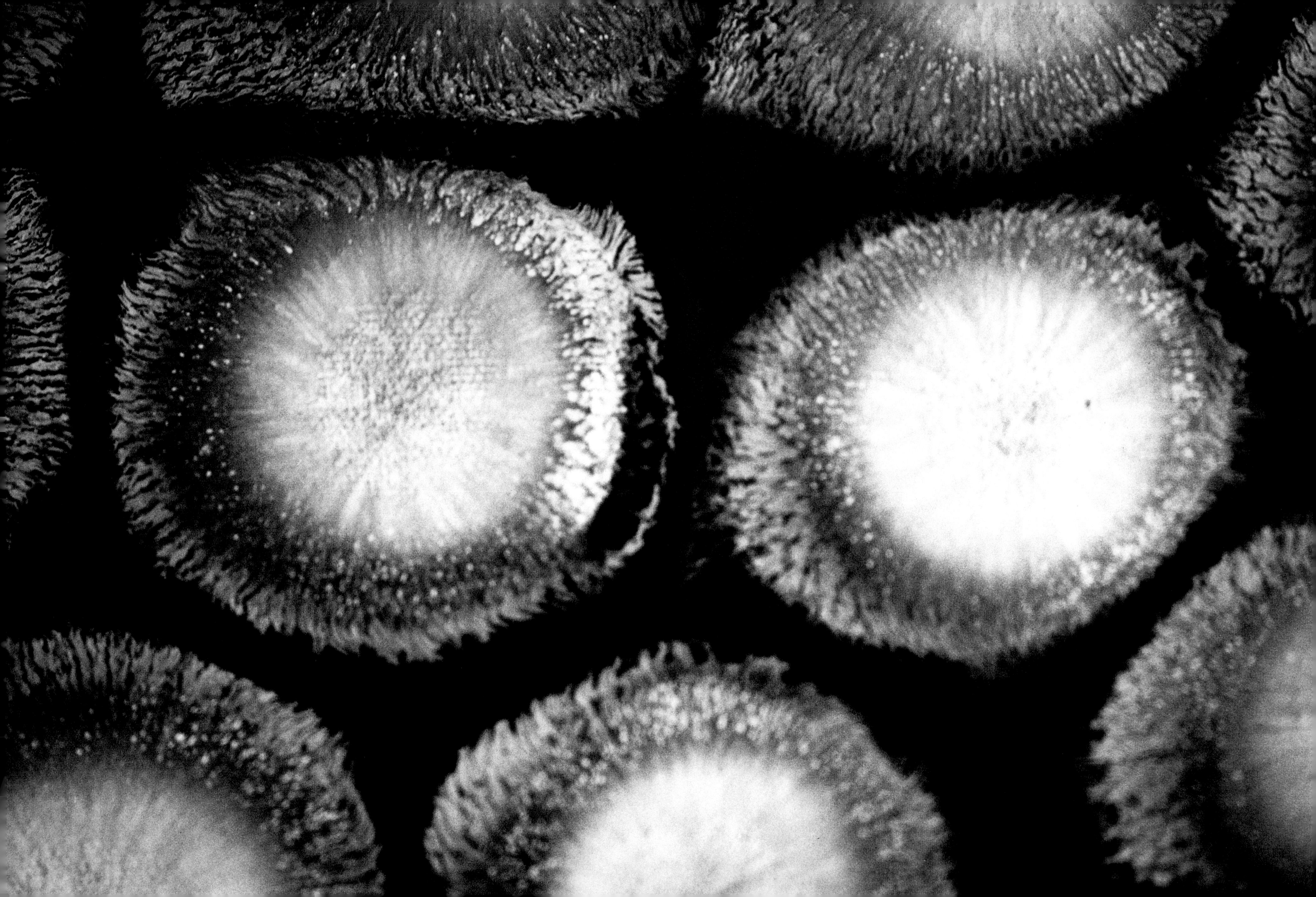

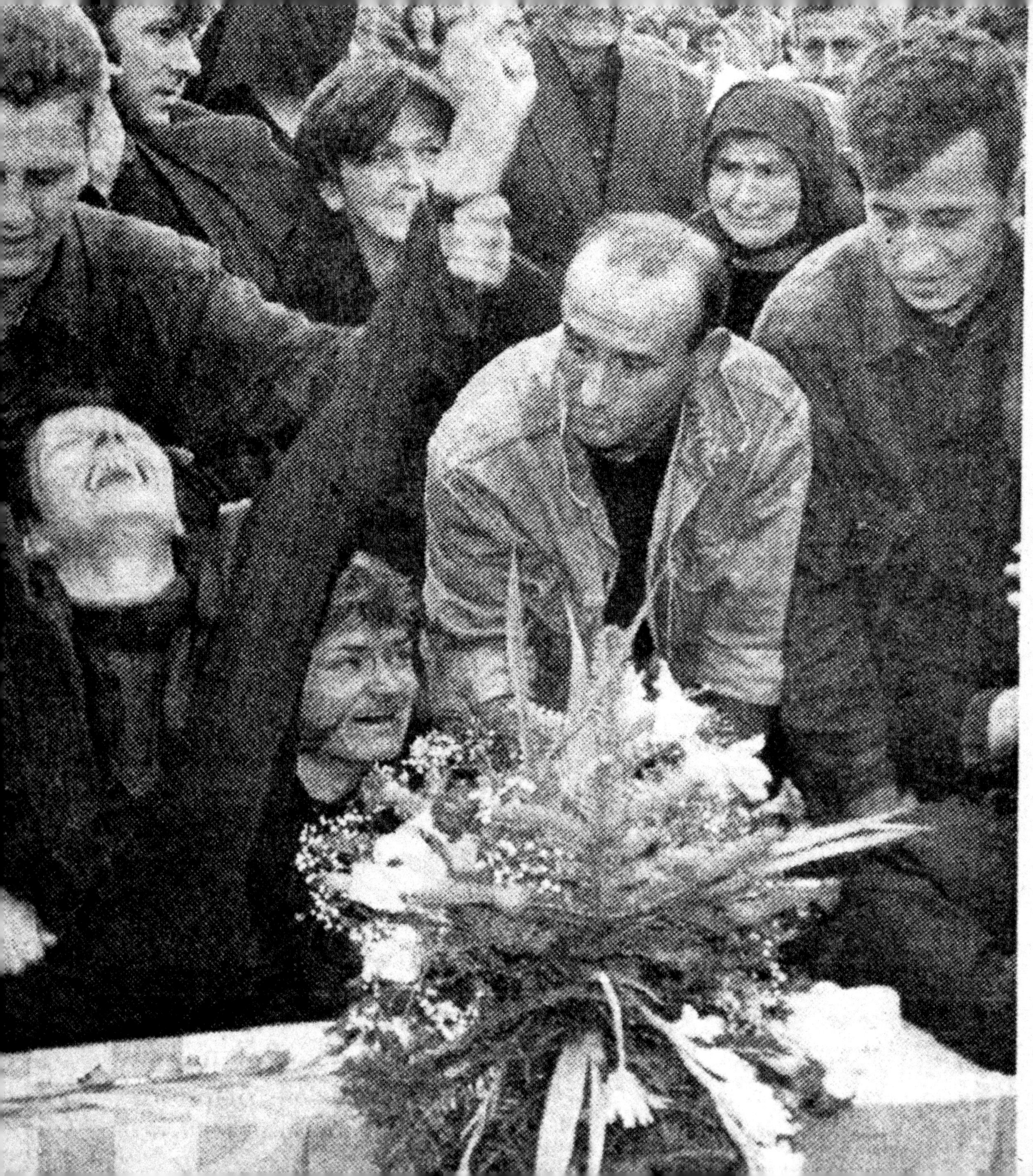

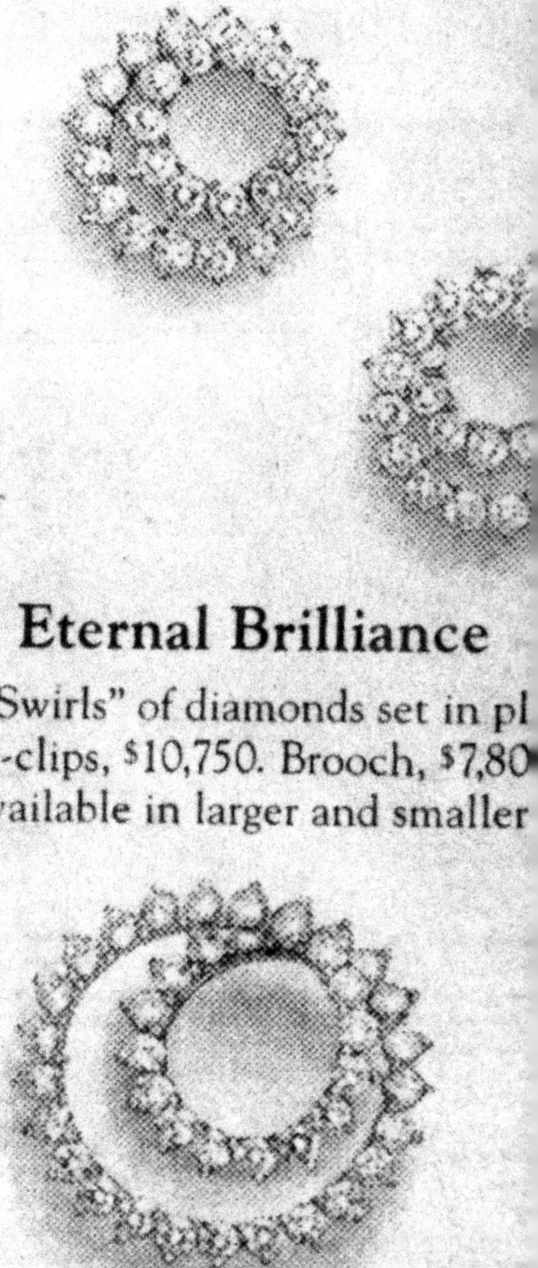

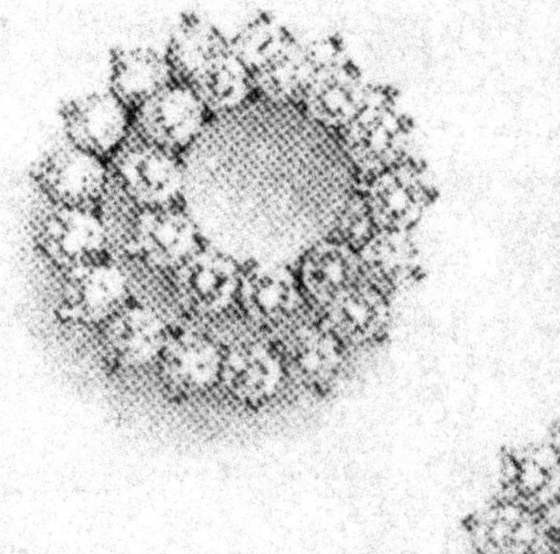

Eternal Brilliance

Tiffany "Swirls" of diamonds set in pl
Ear-clips, $10,750. Brooch, $7,80
Also available in larger and smaller

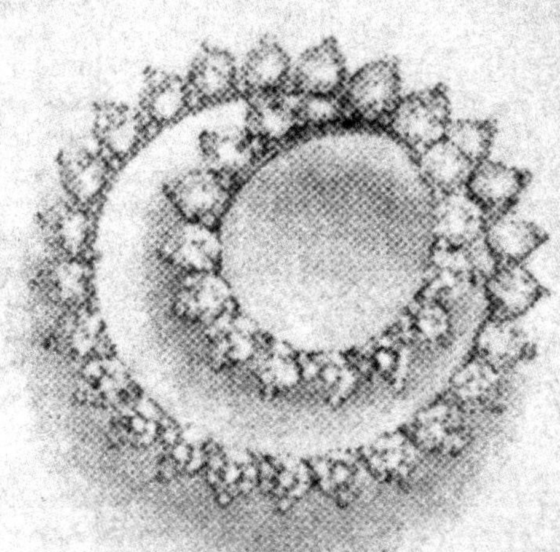

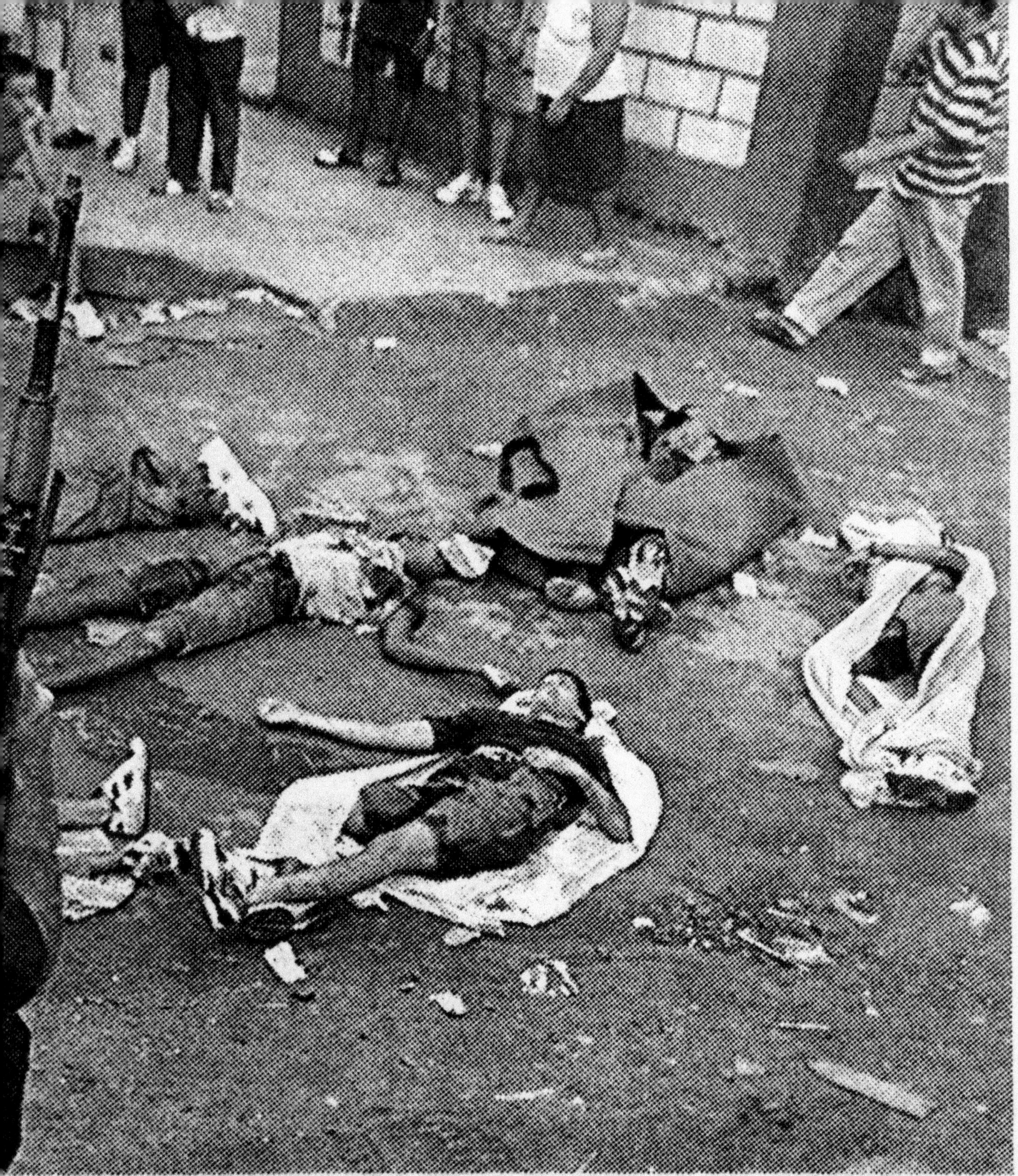

Agence France-Presse

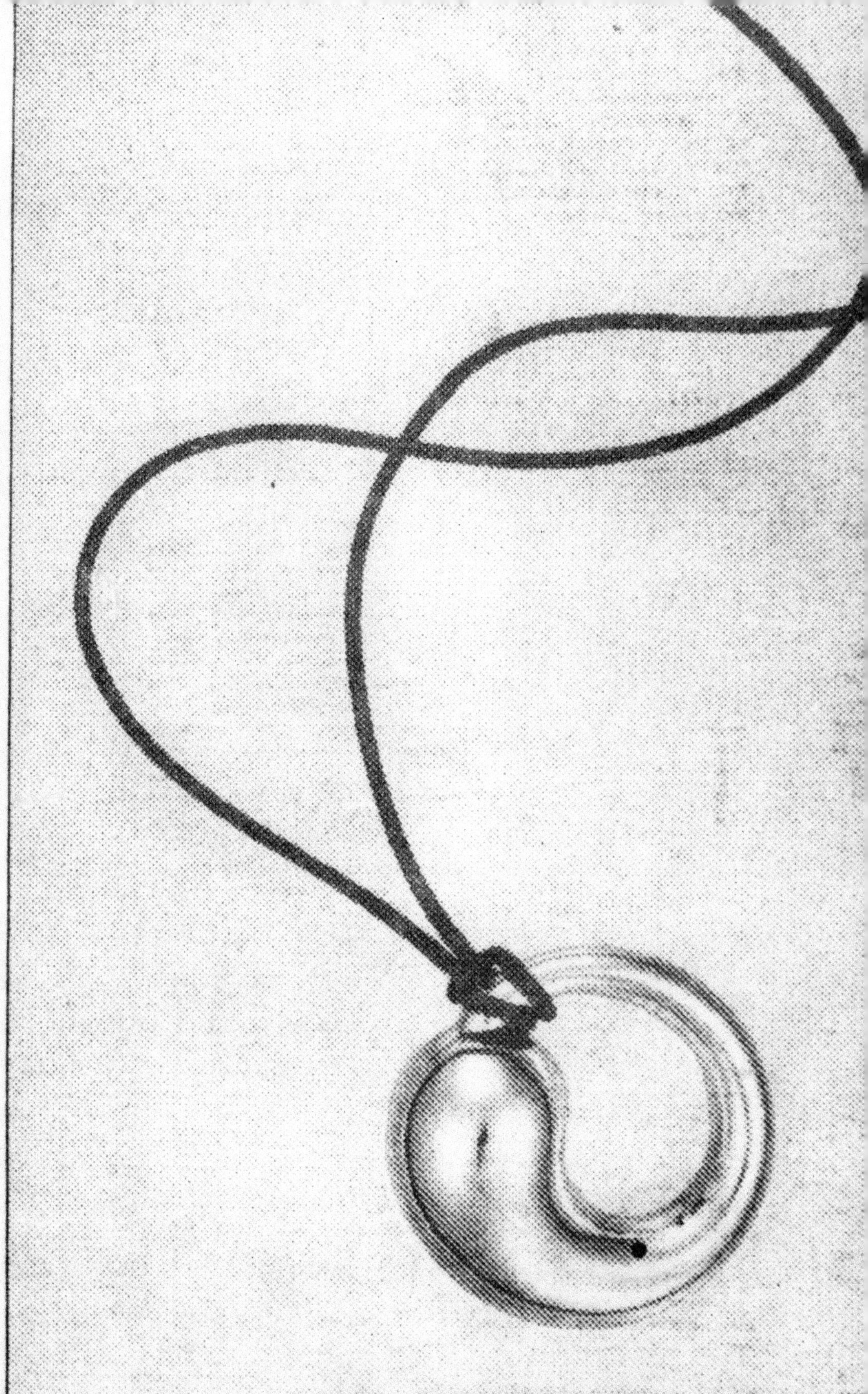

Elsa Peretti's Eternal Cir

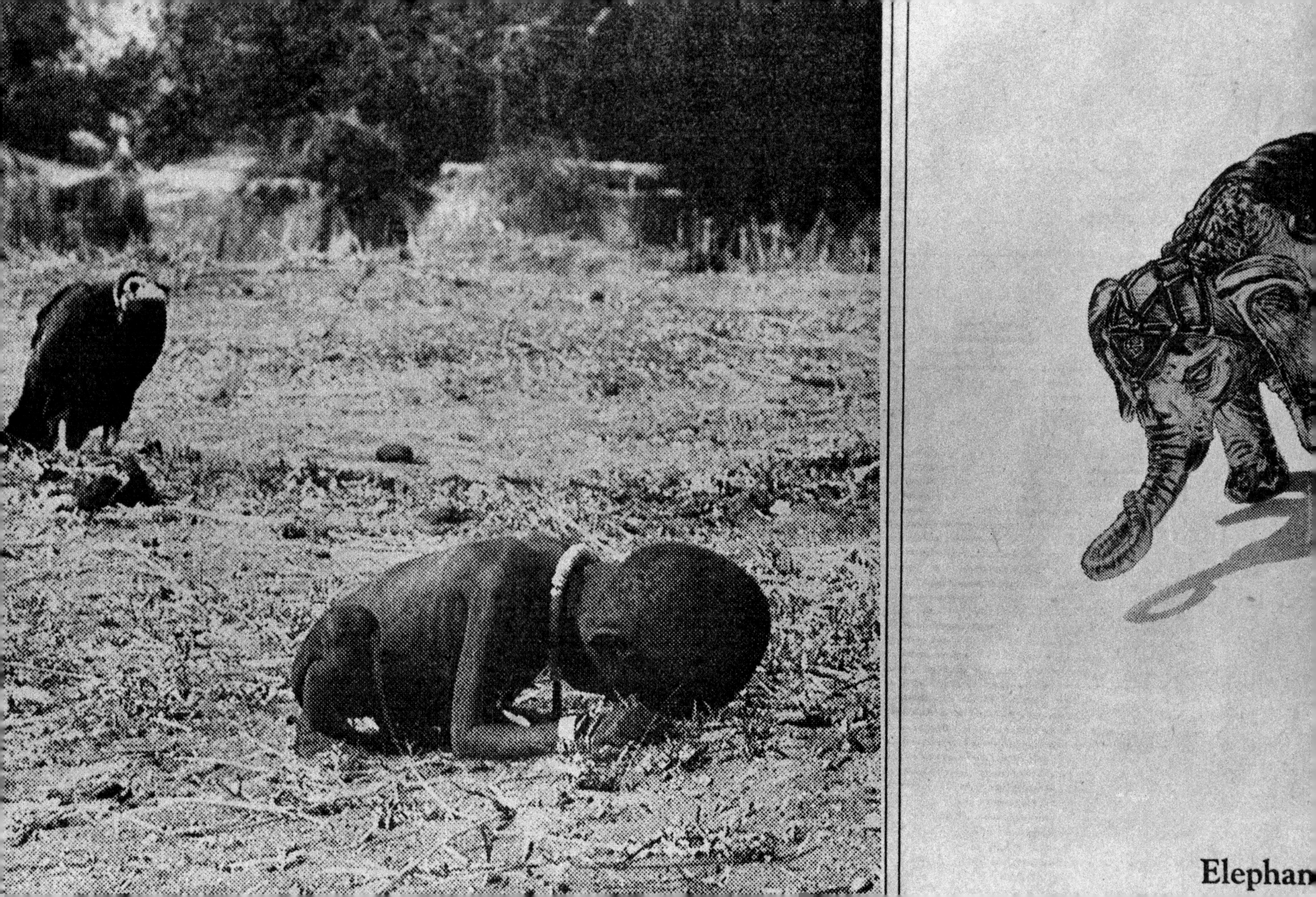
Elephan

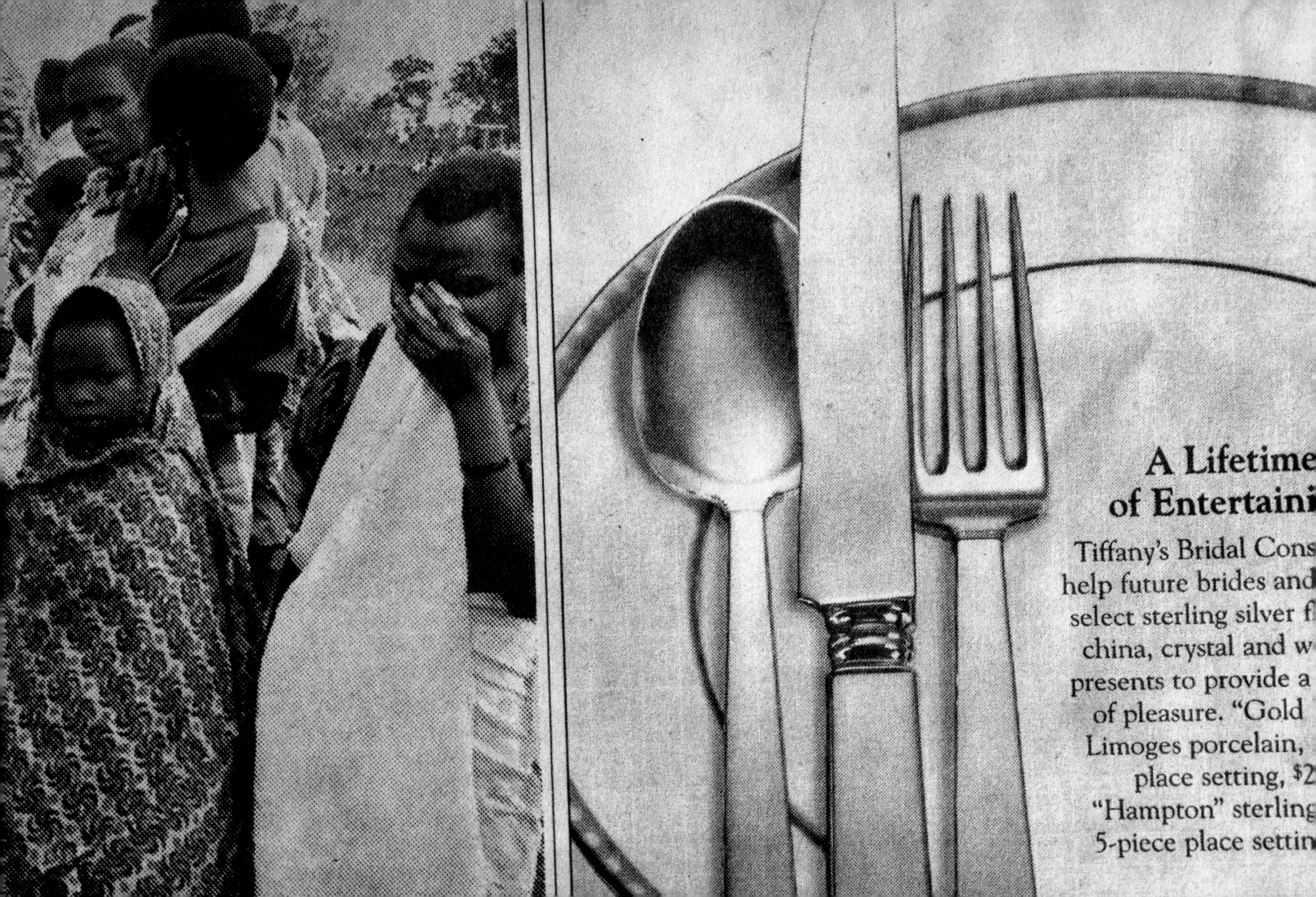

A Lifetime
of Entertaini
Tiffany's Bridal Cons
help future brides and
select sterling silver f
china, crystal and w
presents to provide a
of pleasure. "Gold
Limoges porcelain,
place setting, $2
"Hampton" sterling
5-piece place settin

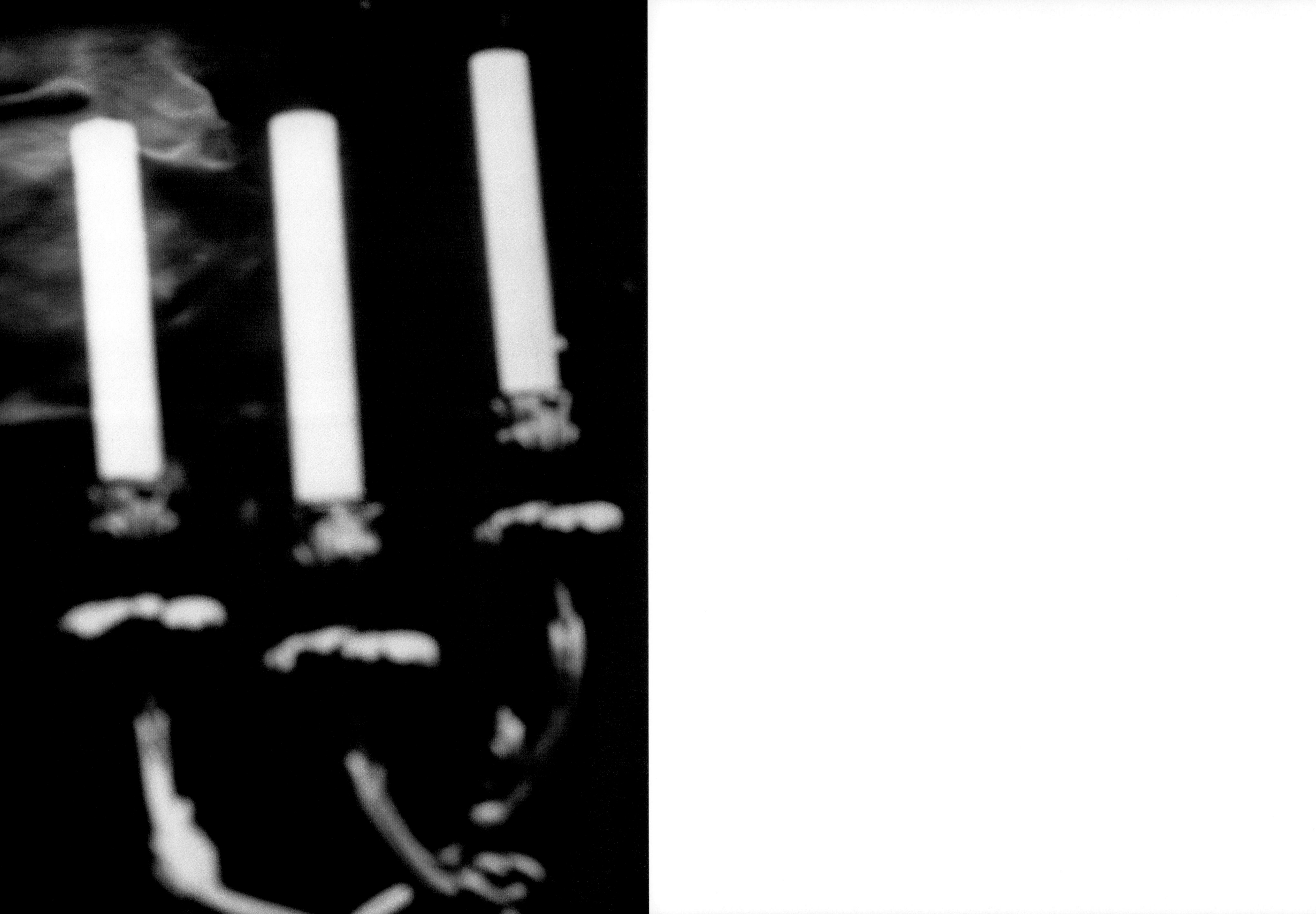

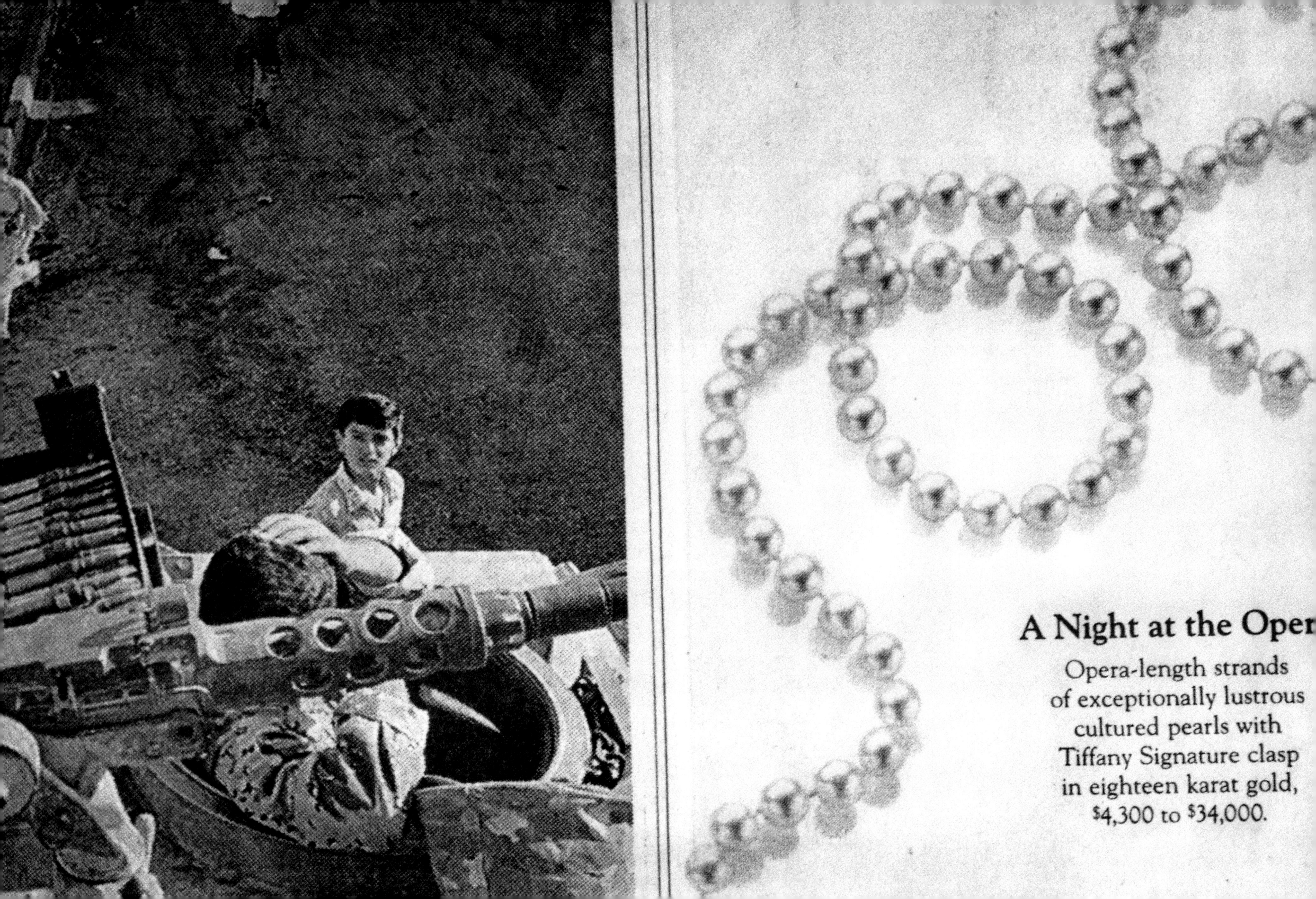
A Night at the Oper
Opera-length strands
of exceptionally lustrous
cultured pearls with
Tiffany Signature clasp
in eighteen karat gold,
$4,300 to $34,000.

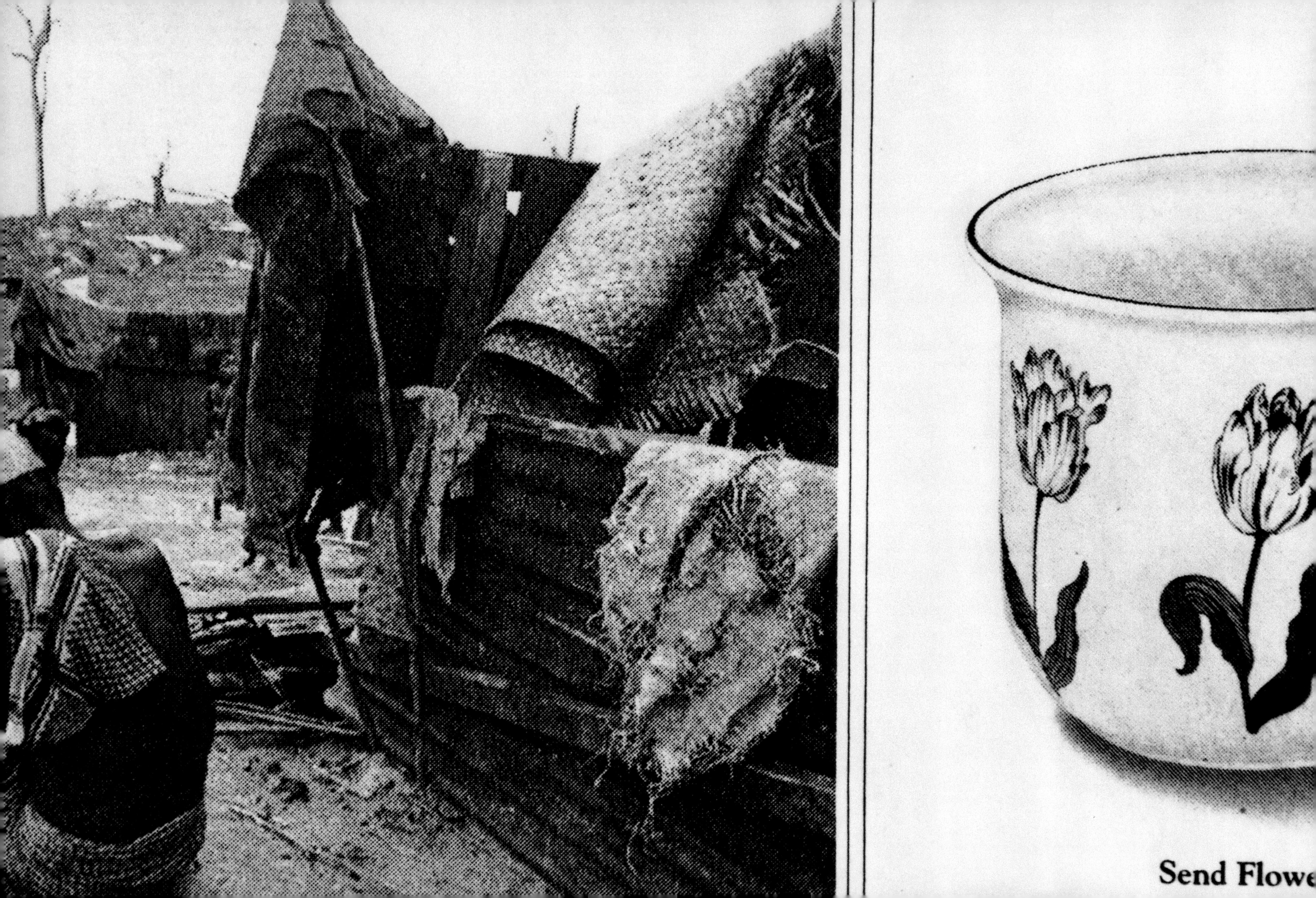
Send Flowe

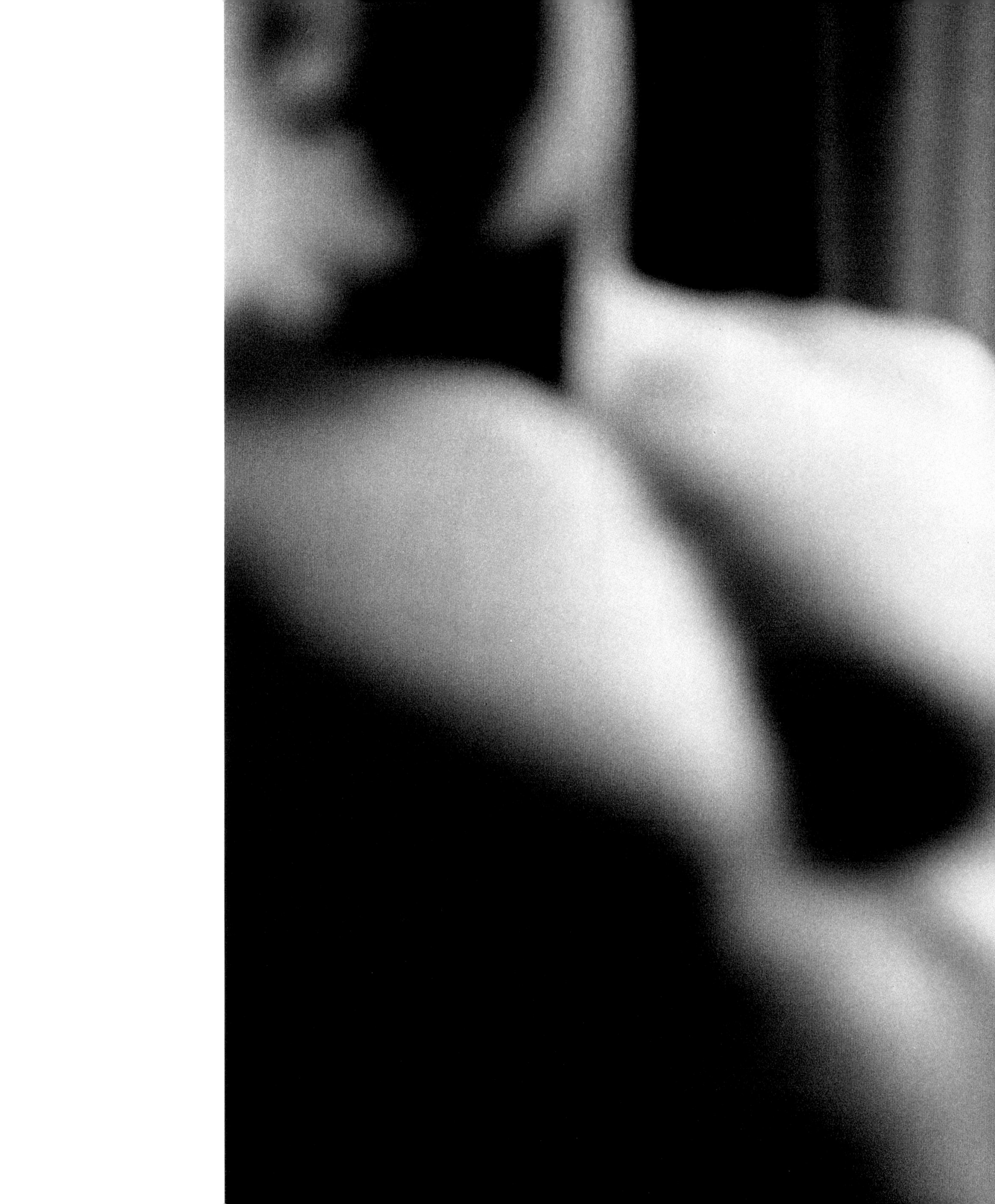

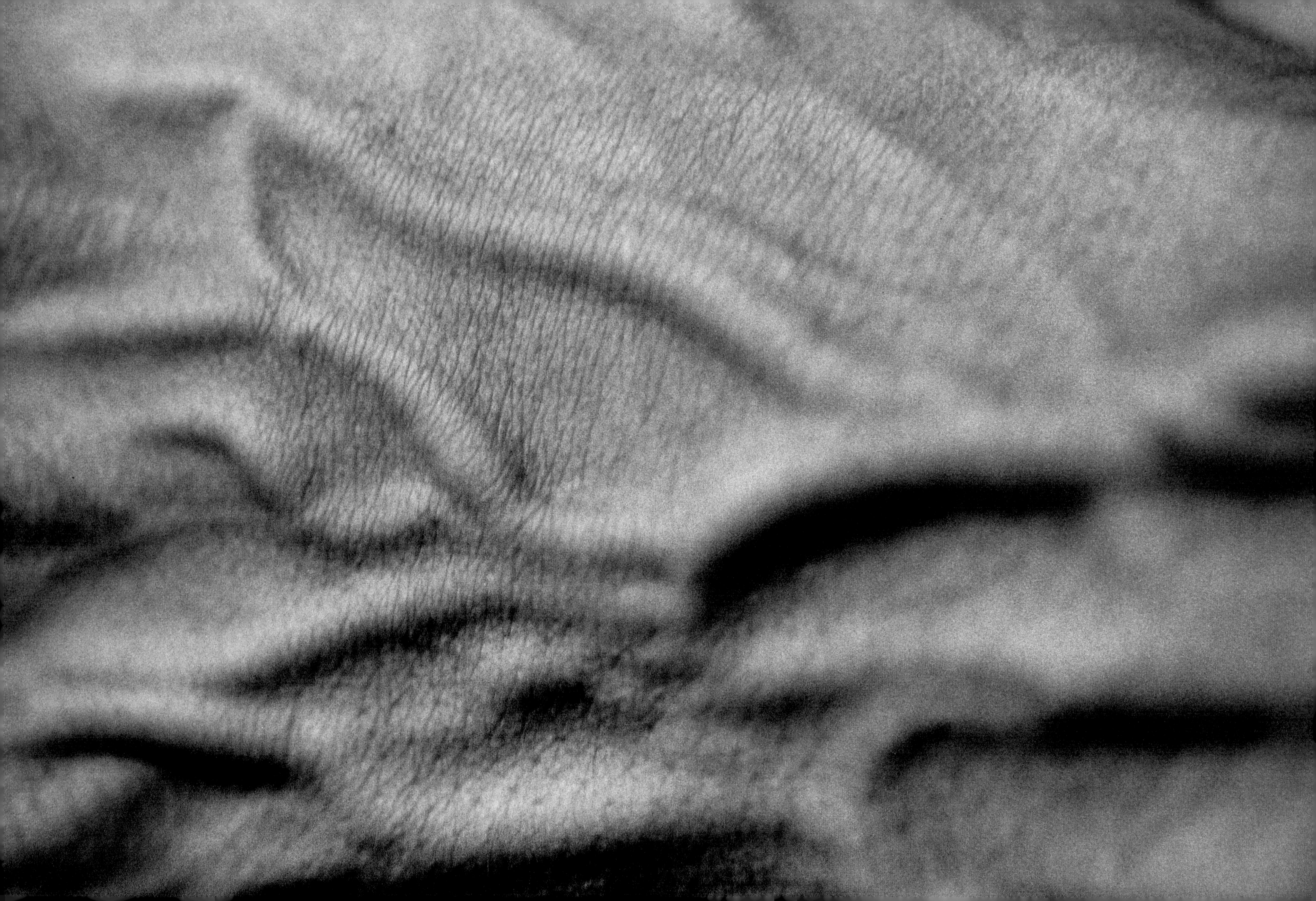

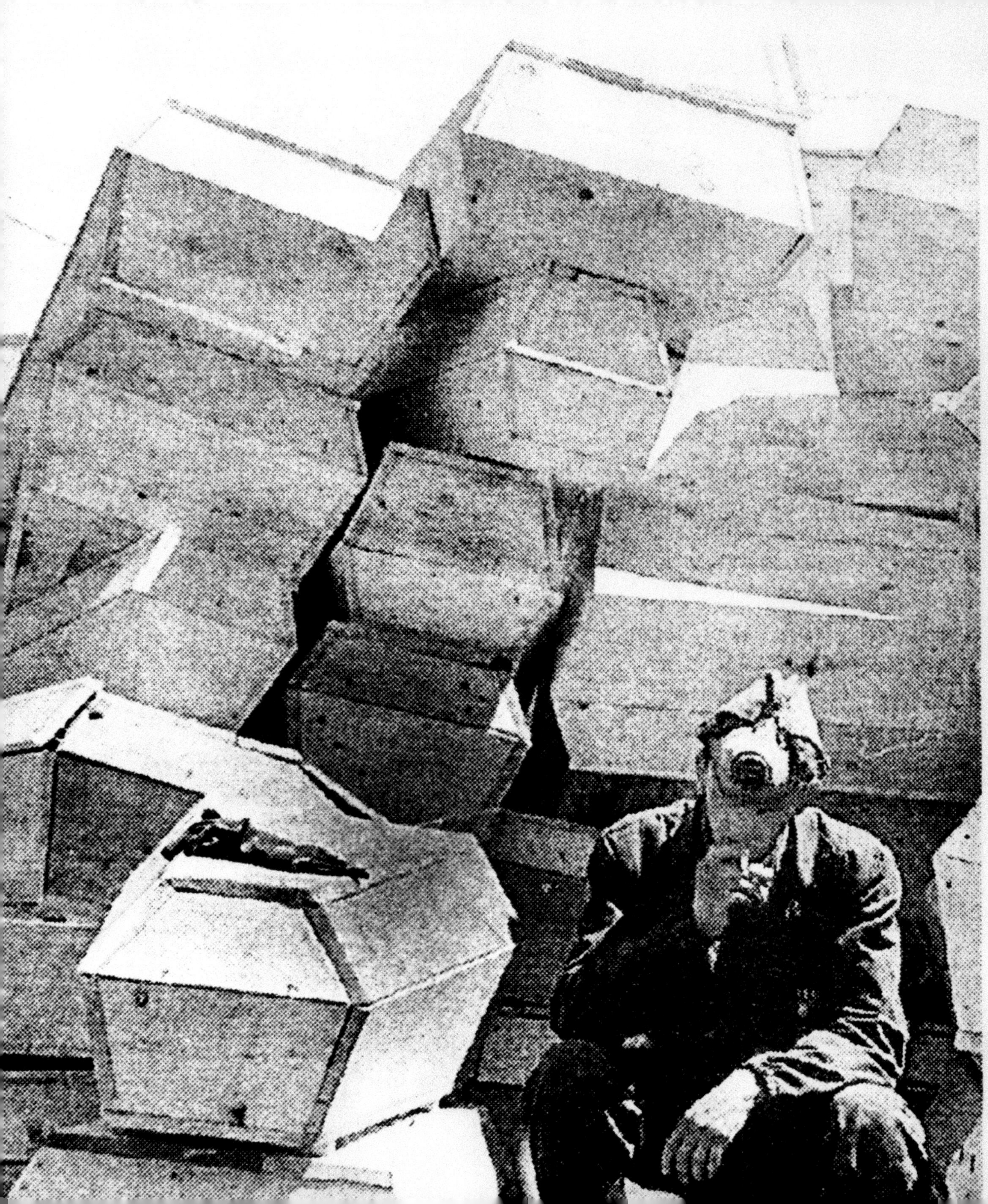

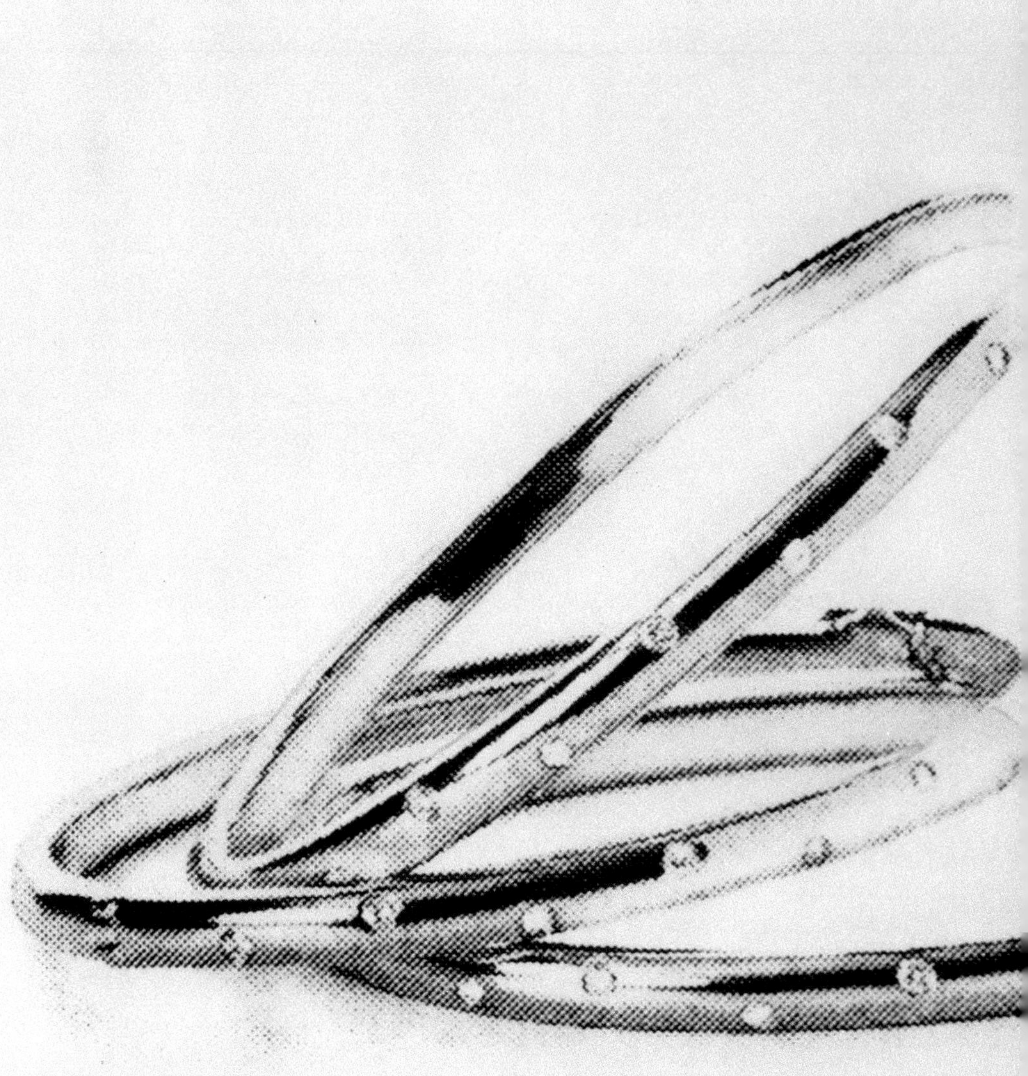

Starlight, Star Bright

"Etoile" designs in eighteen kara
gold with diamonds set in platin

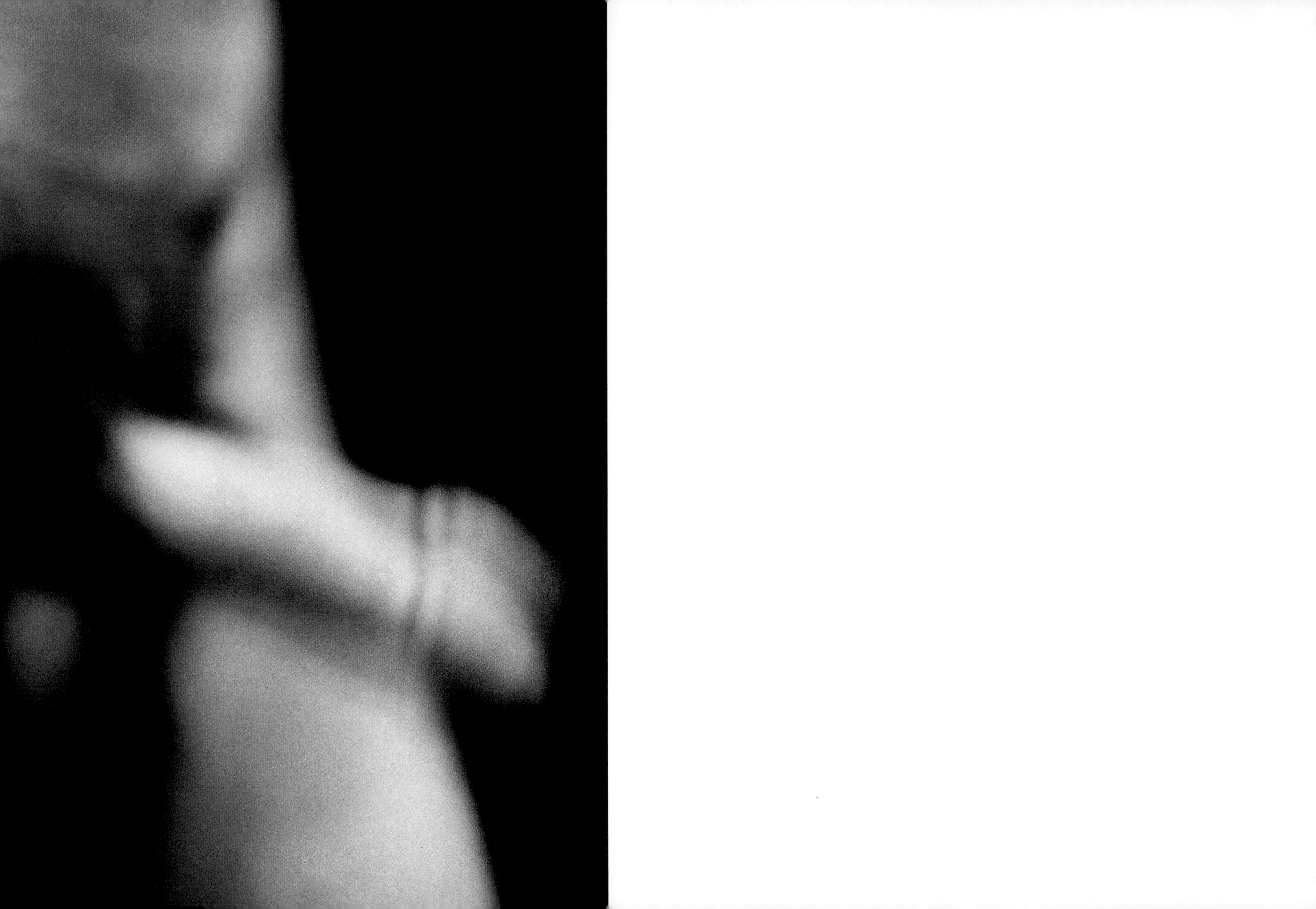

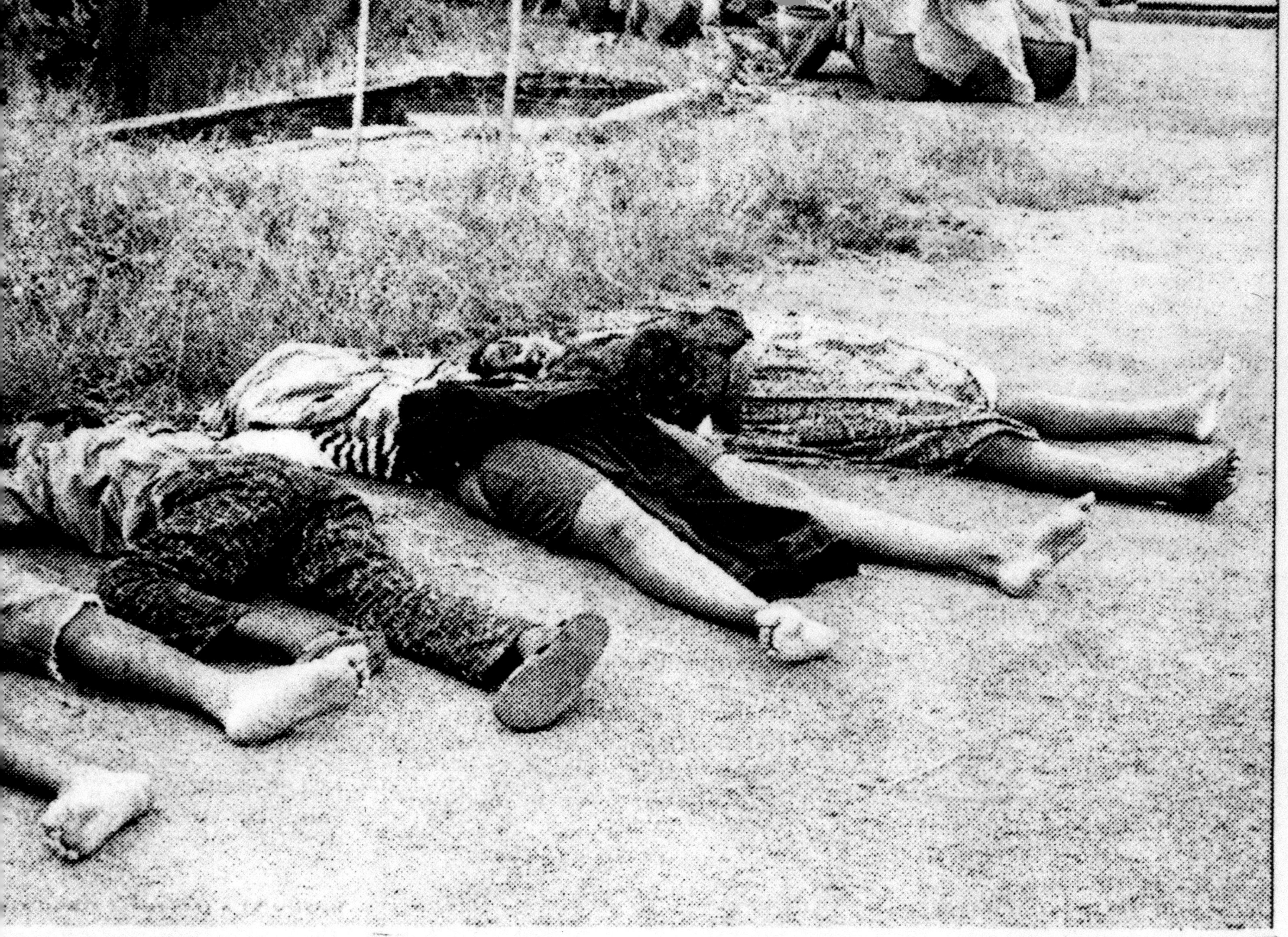

Reuters

sands have died, lay beside the street yesterday in the center of Kigali, the capital.

ys It Is Powerless to Halt the Violence

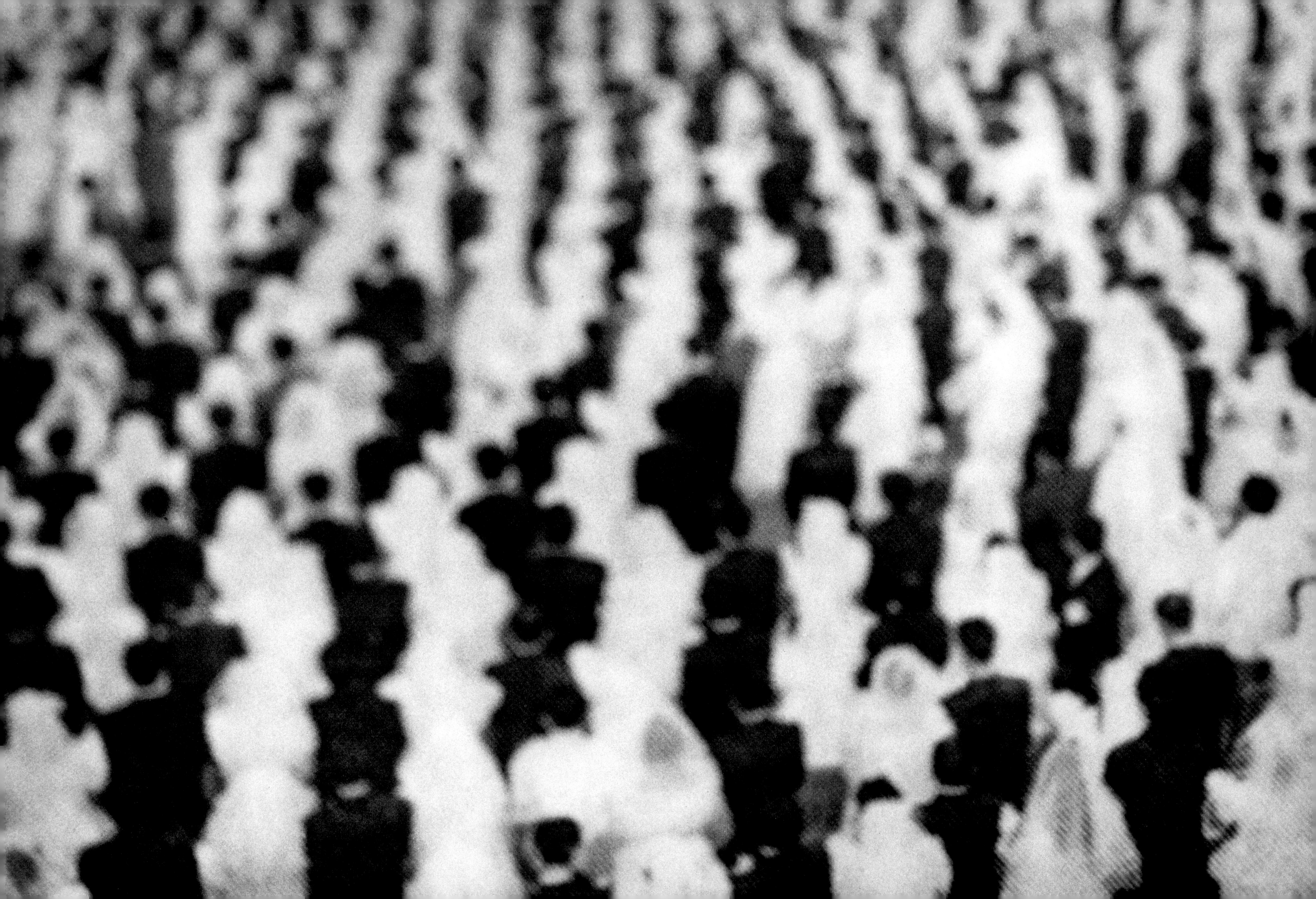

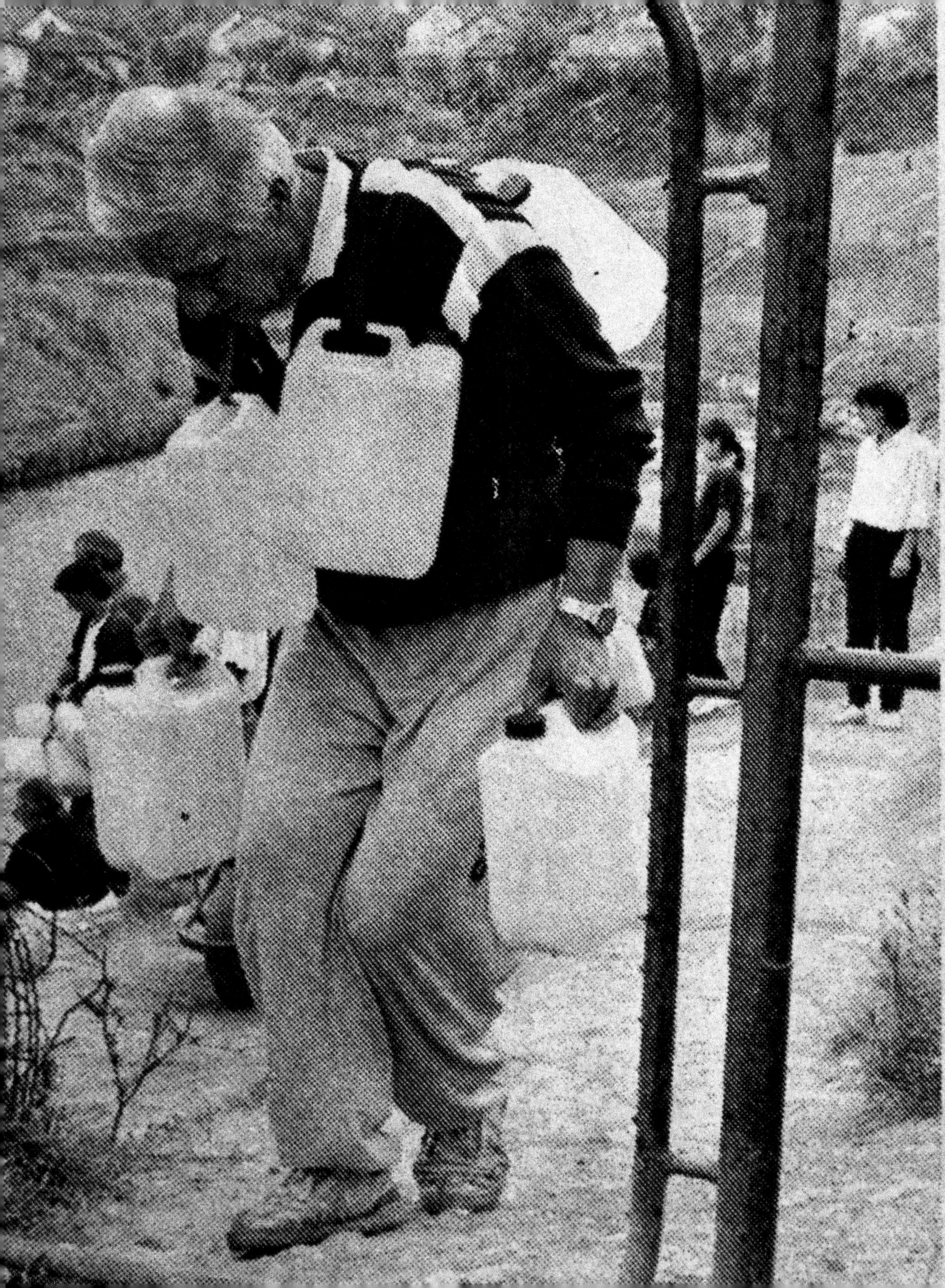

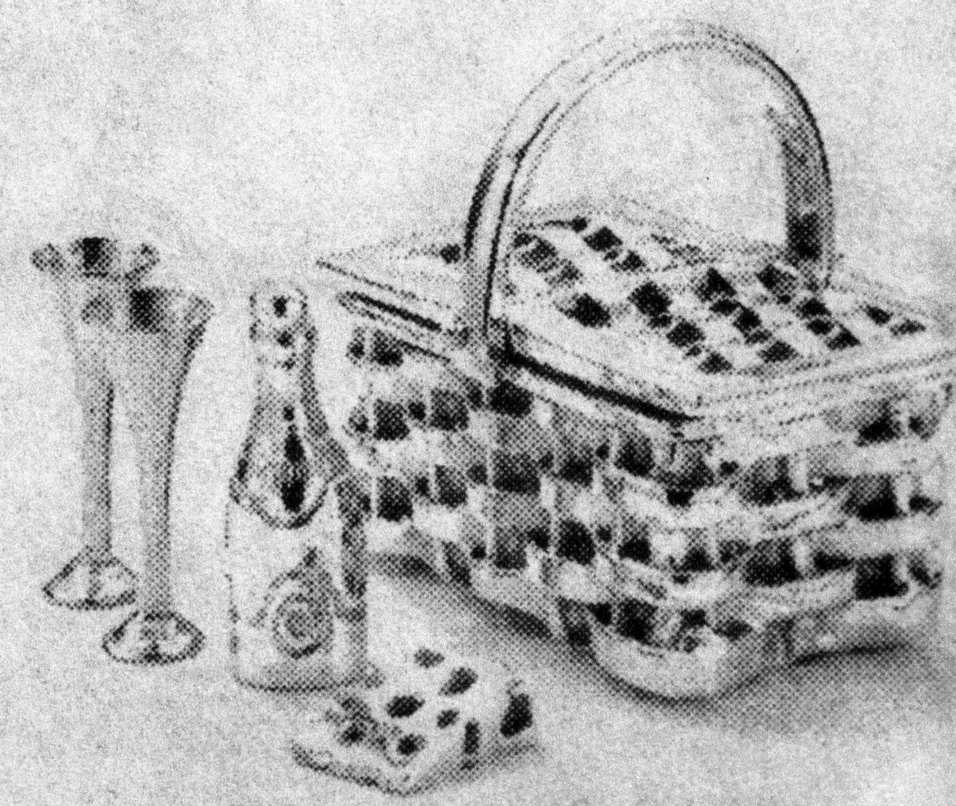

Picnic in the Park

Miniature "Picnic Basket" in
sterling silver with champagne bottle,
flutes and cheese, $375.

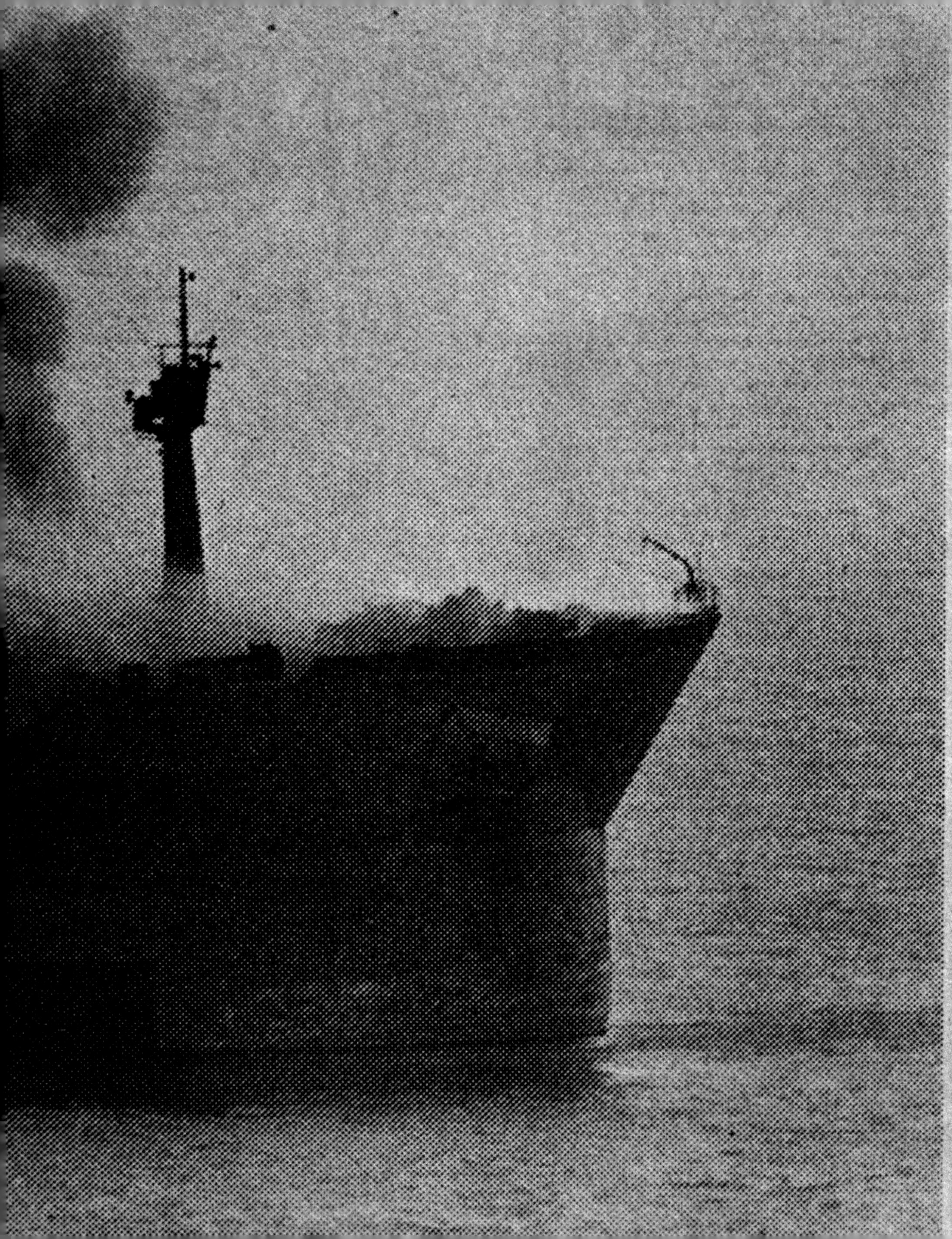

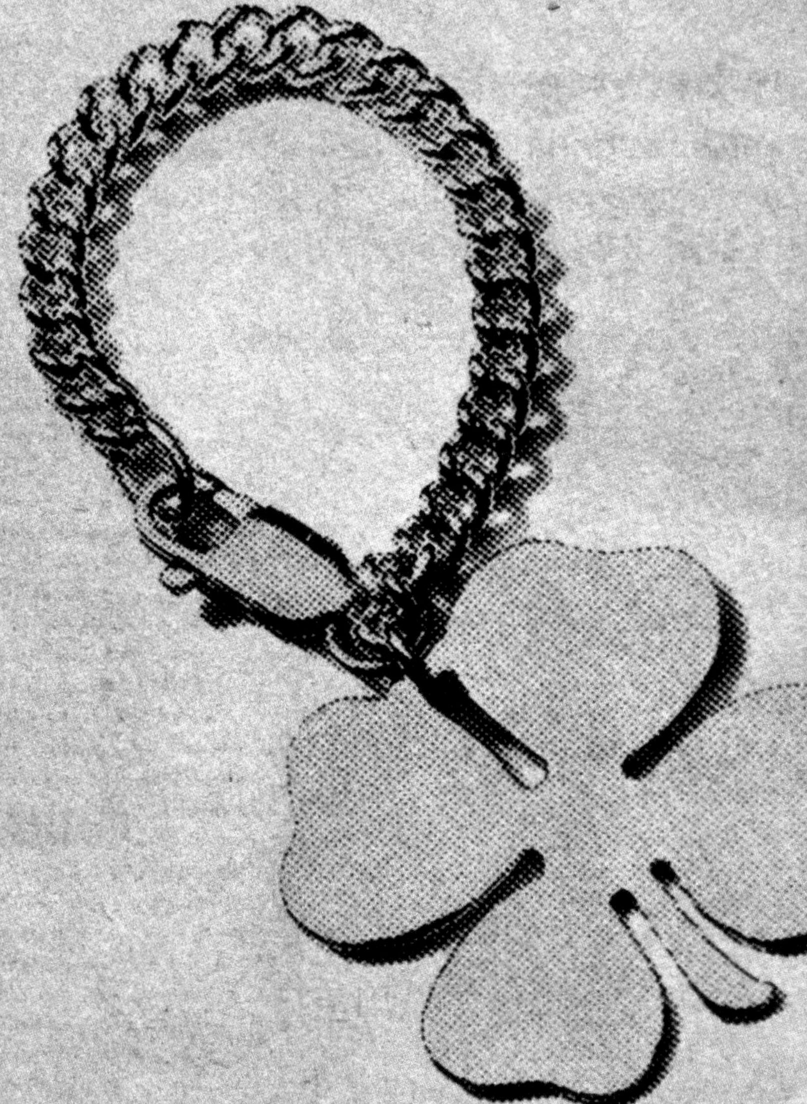

Four-leaf clover key chain from Tiffan
collection of sterling silver accessories,
To order, please call 800-526-0649.

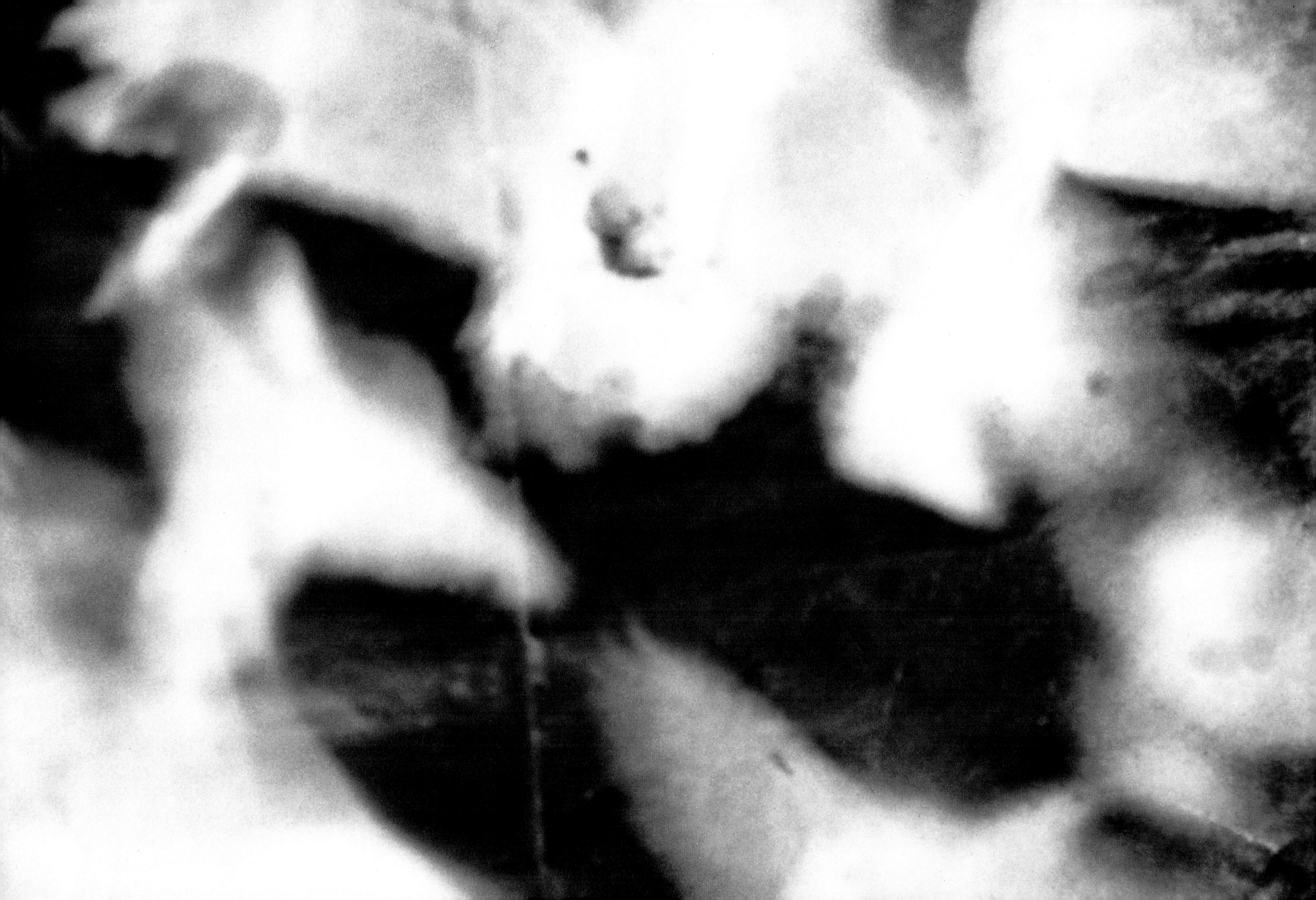

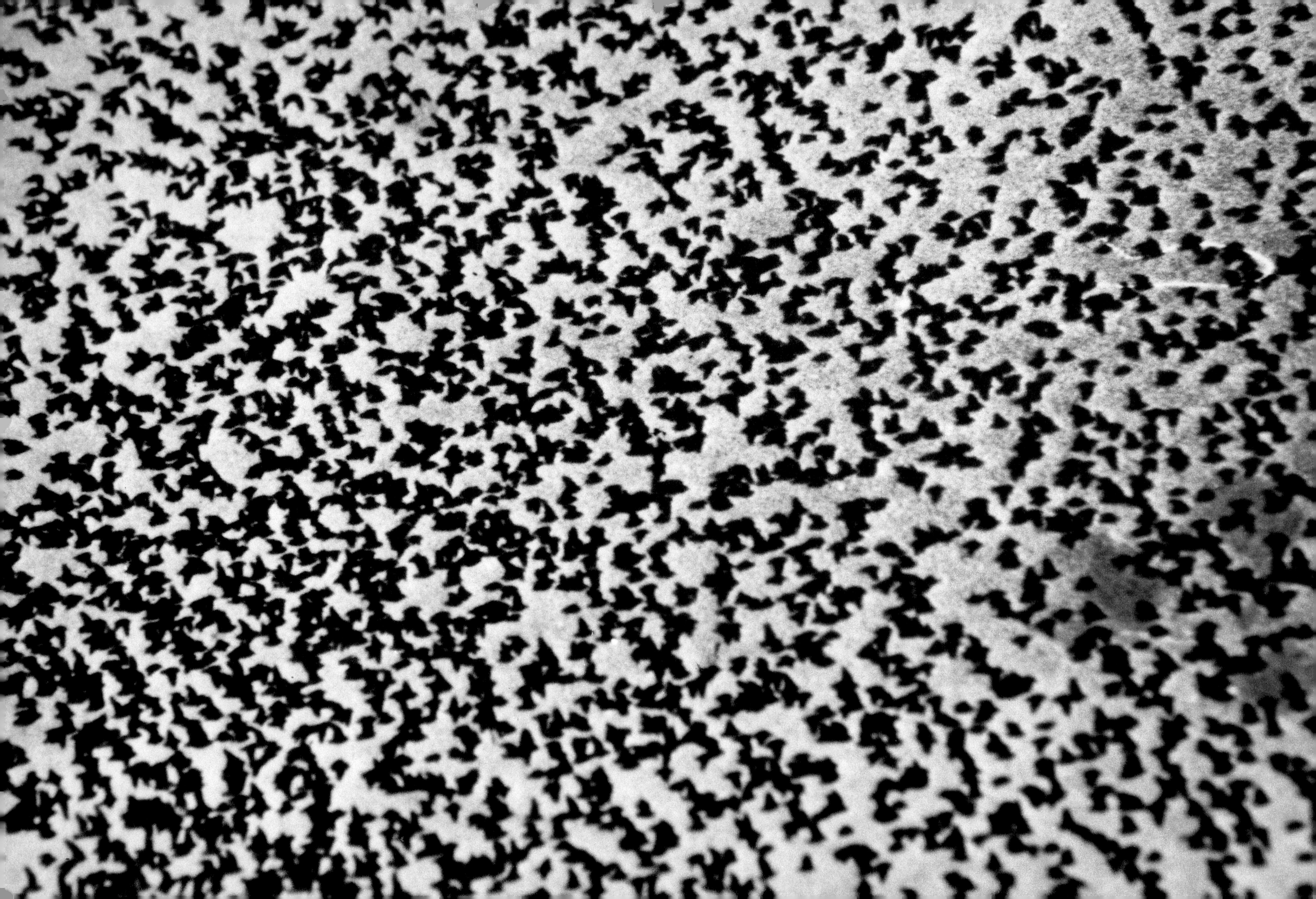

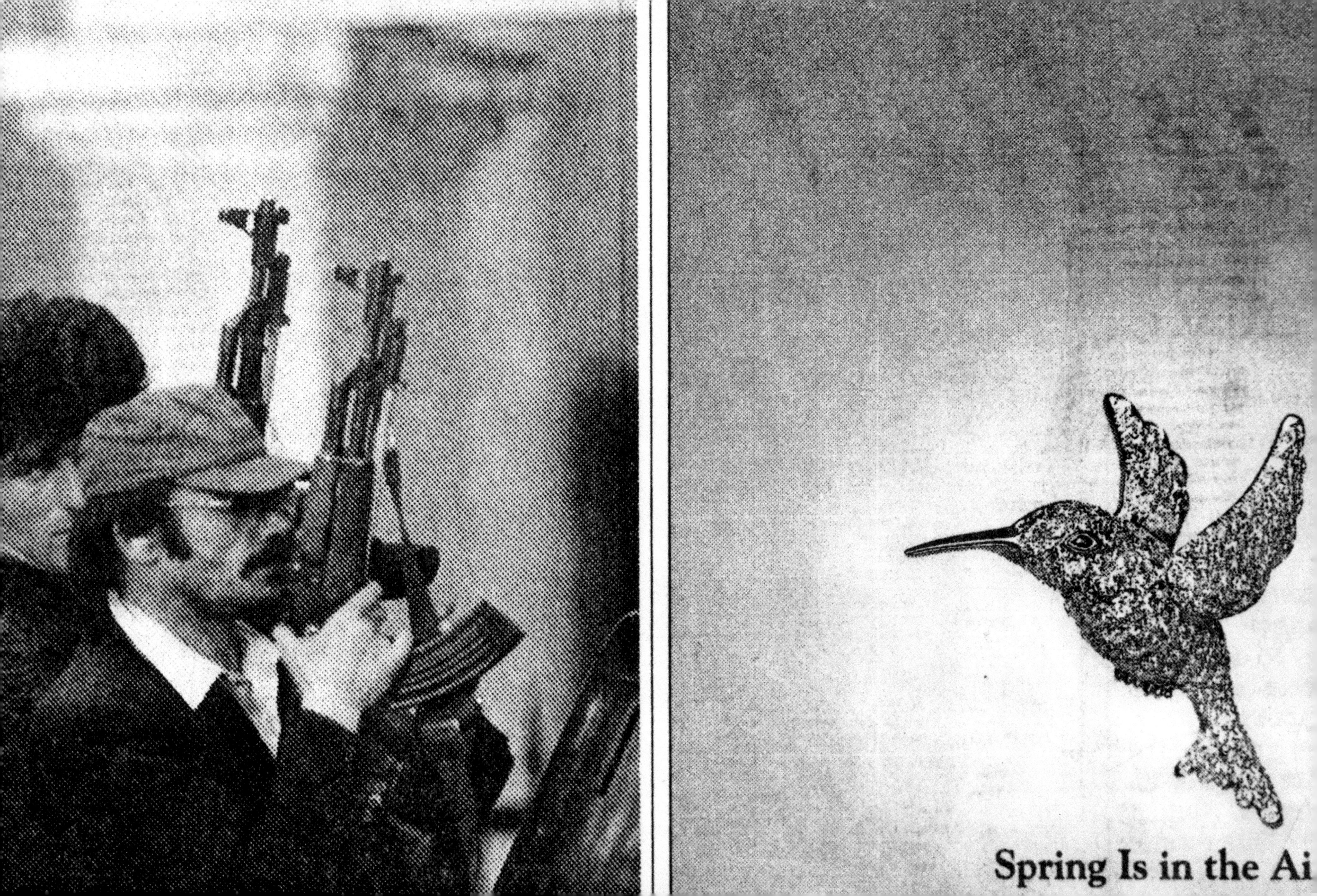

Spring Is in the Ai

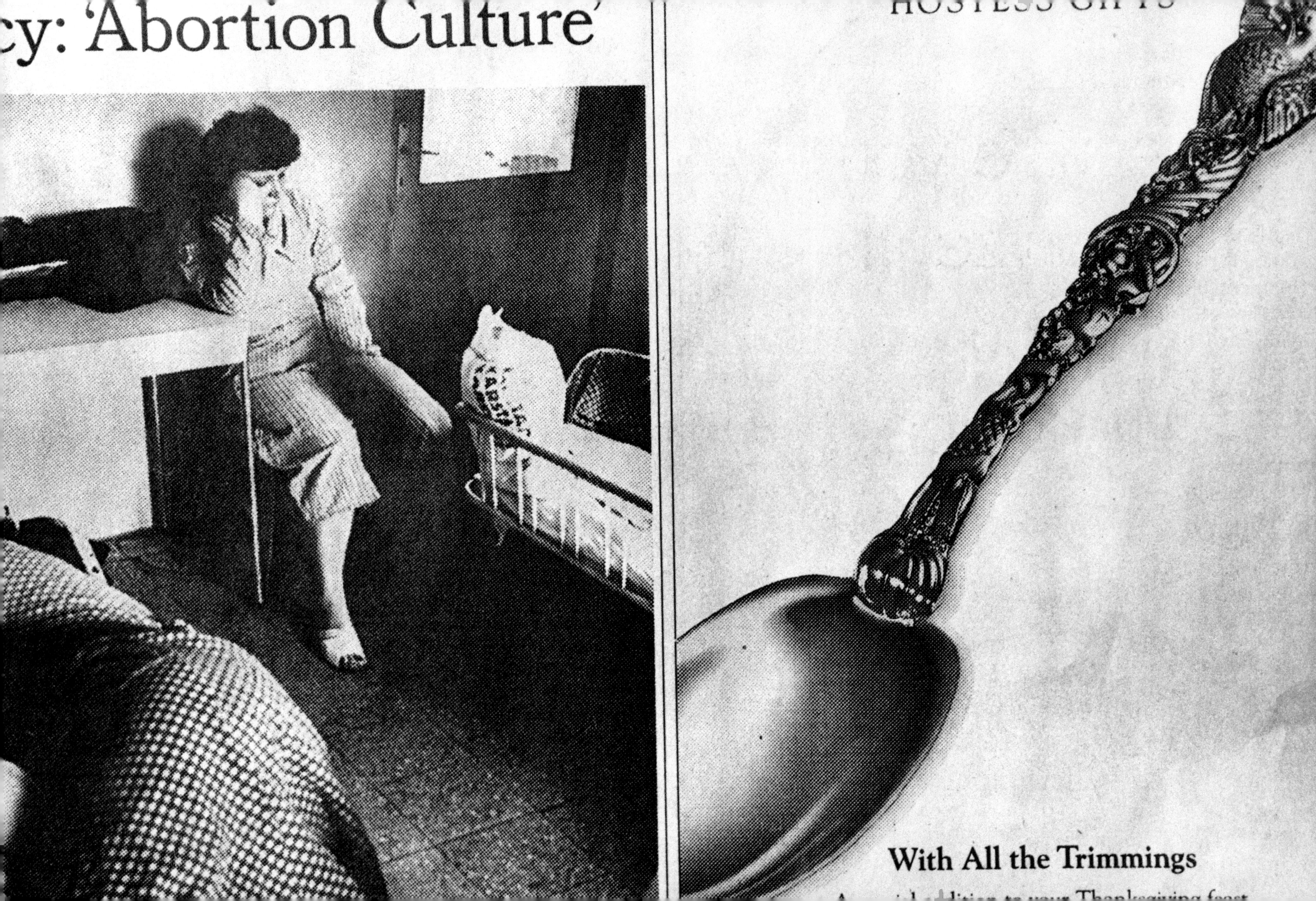

cy: 'Abortion Culture'

HOSTESS GIFTS

With All the Trimmings

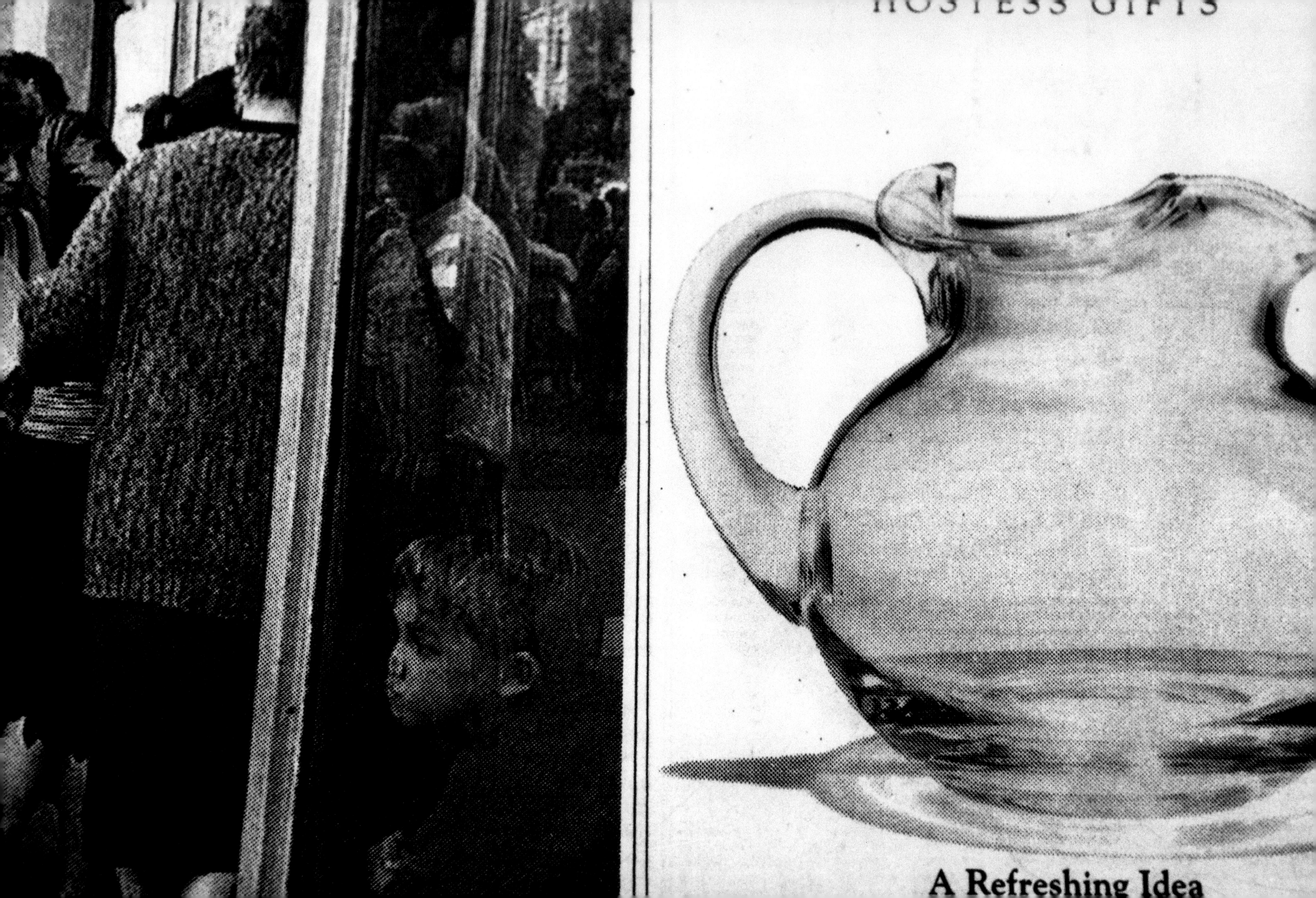

HOSTESS GIFTS
A Refreshing Idea

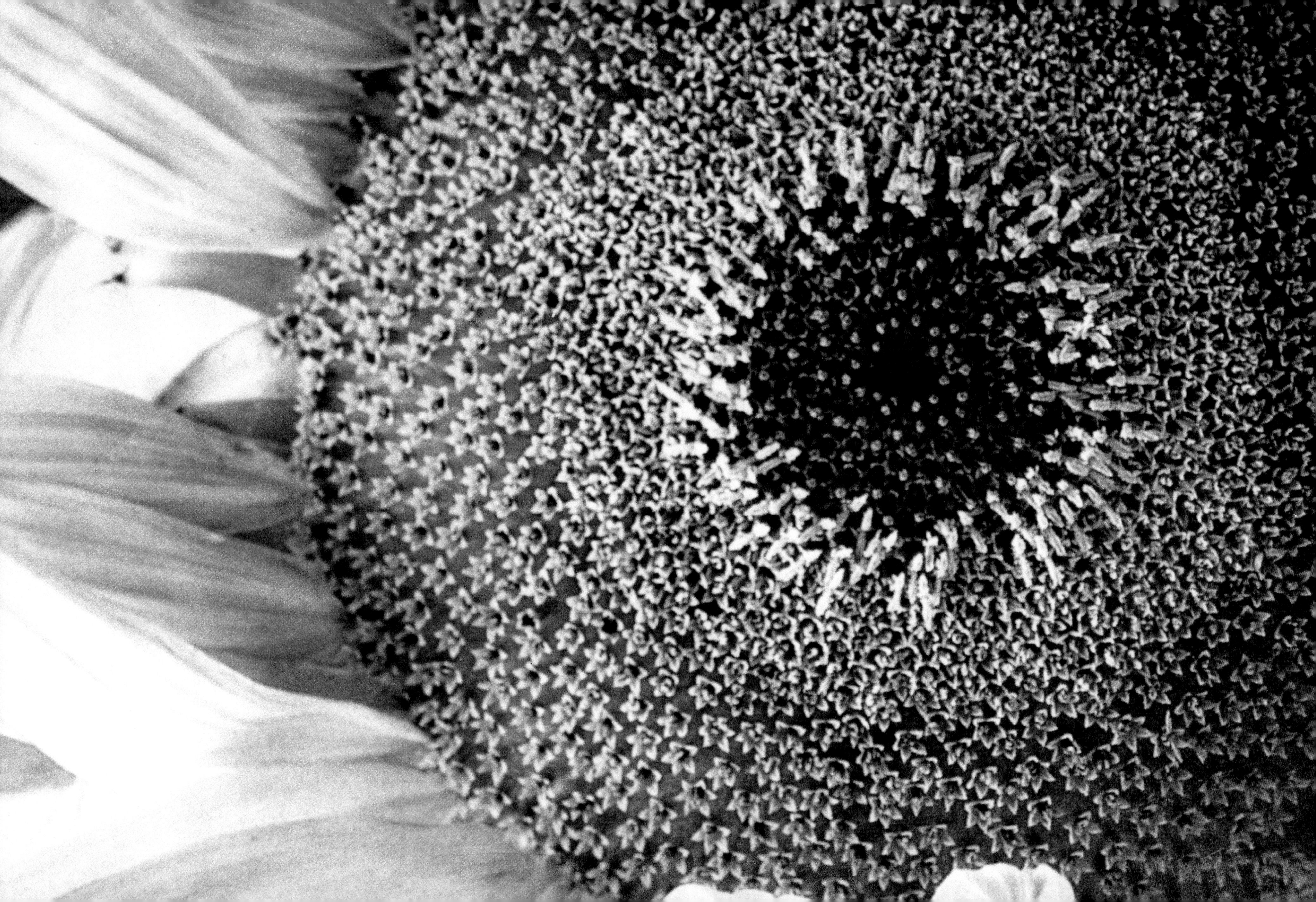

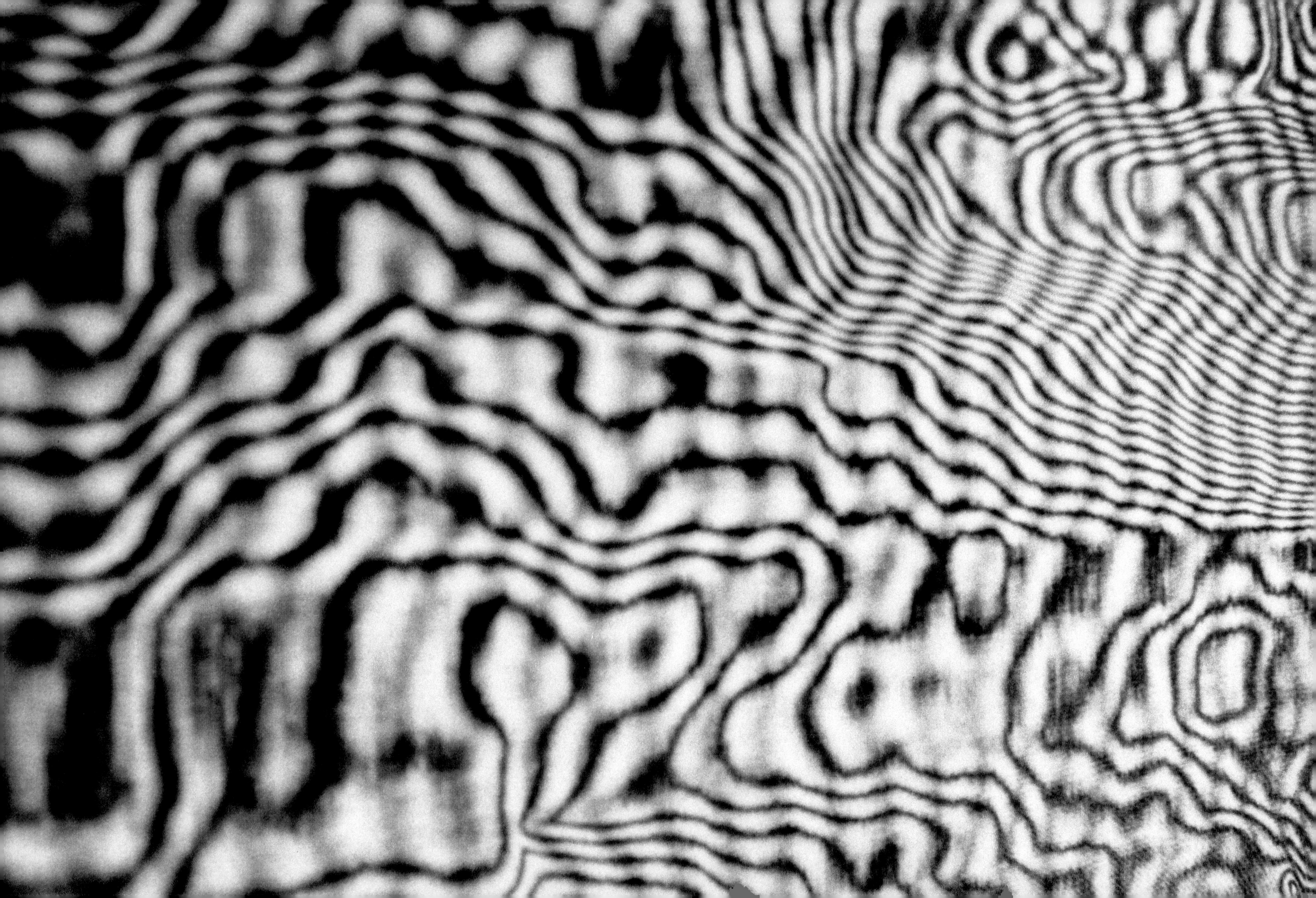

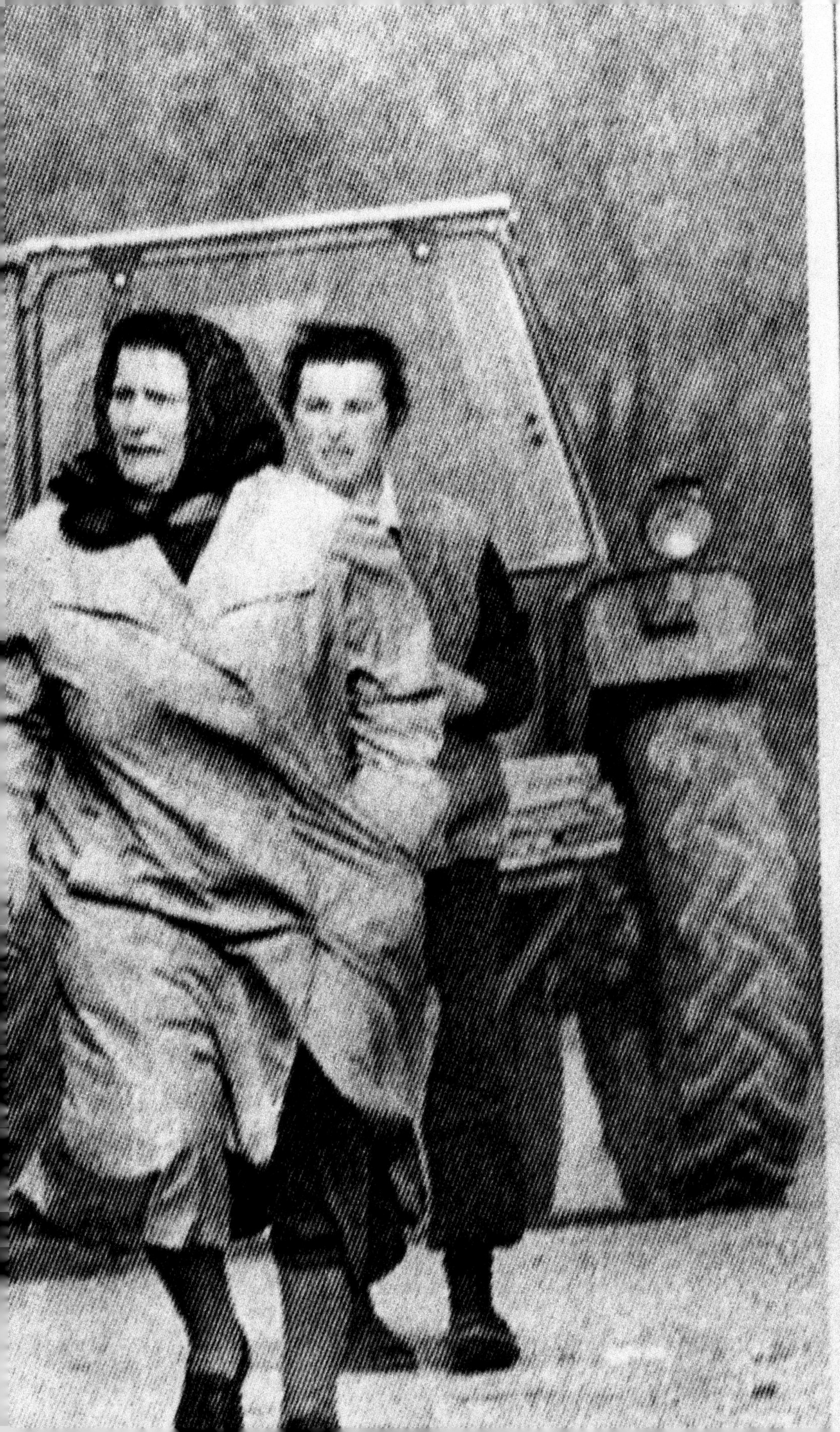

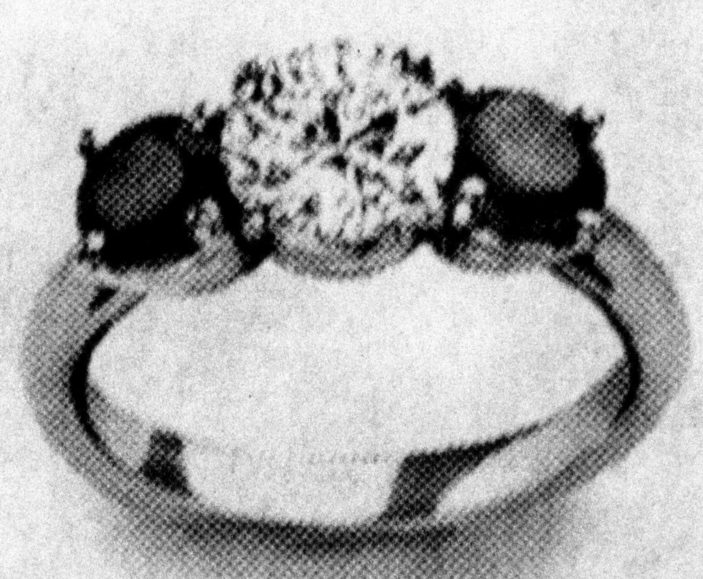

Somebody's Smitten

Diamonds, sapphires, emeralds
or rubies of exceptional quality,
perfectly matched and set in
platinum or eighteen karat gold.
For less than you may imagine,

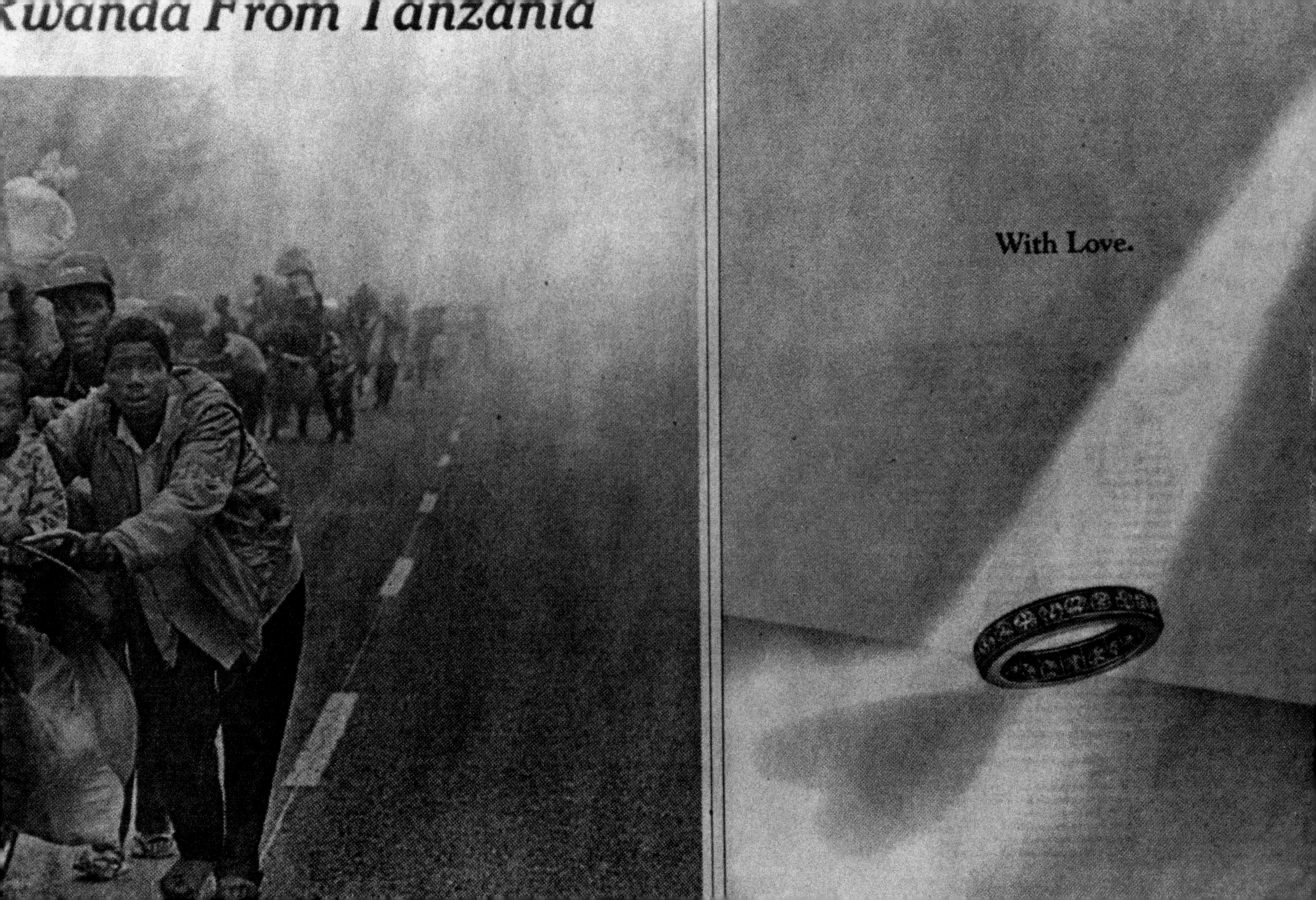
Rwanda From Tanzania
With Love.

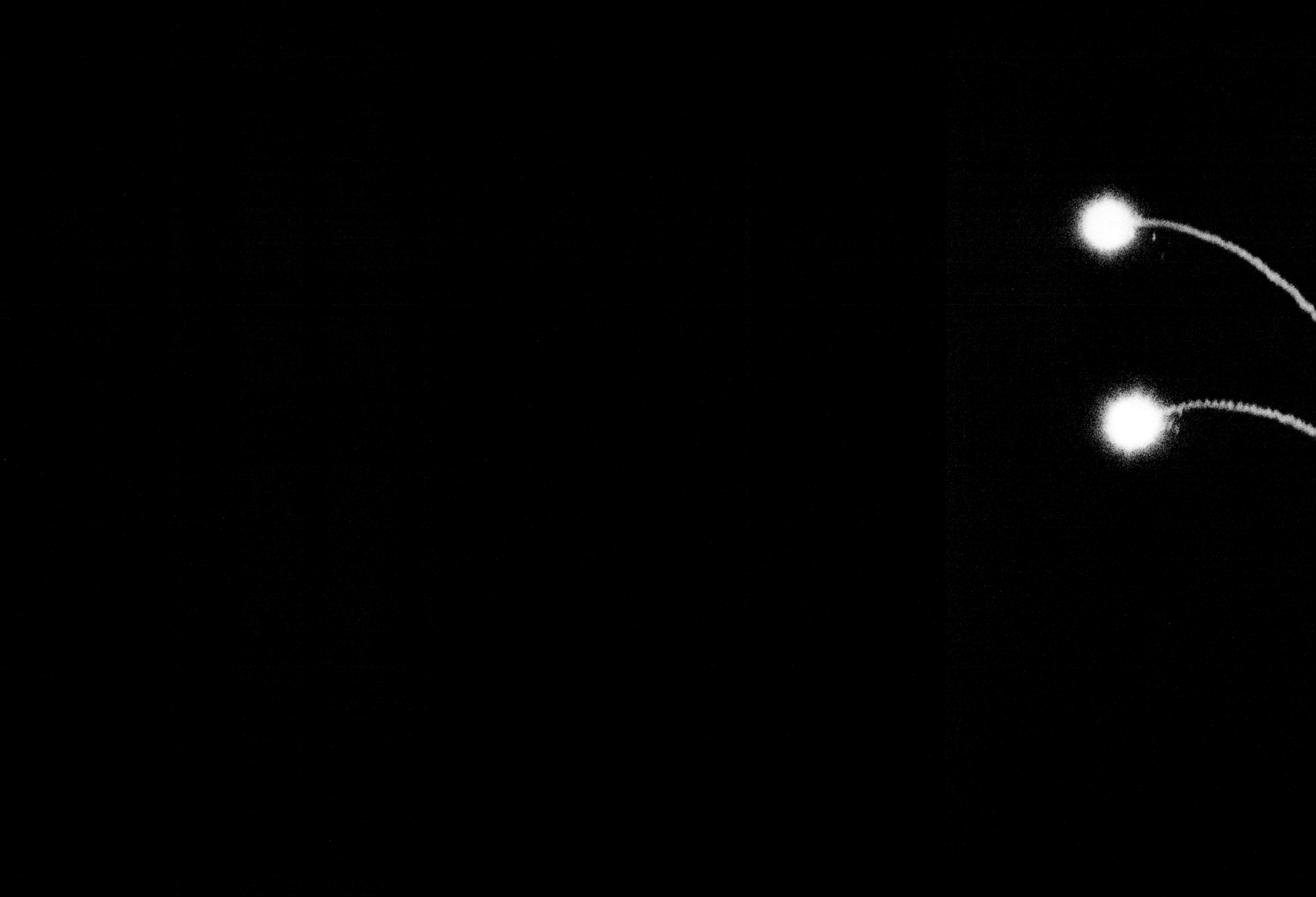

rock sentiment toward life," he writes. "For Jews, it is a sense of compelling duty," and for Christians, "a sense of overwhelming gratitude."

No one can offer generalizations like this without arousing strong r

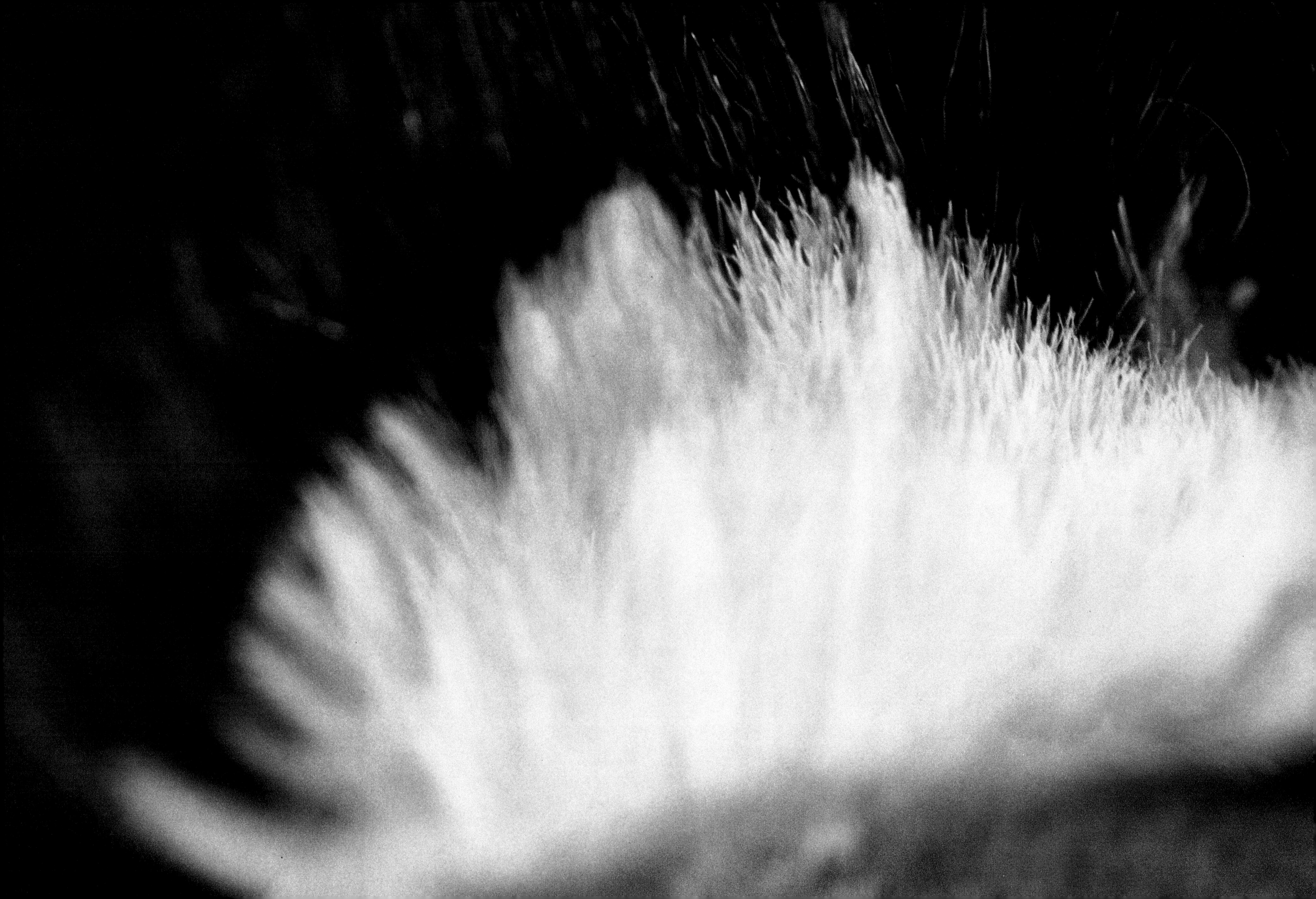

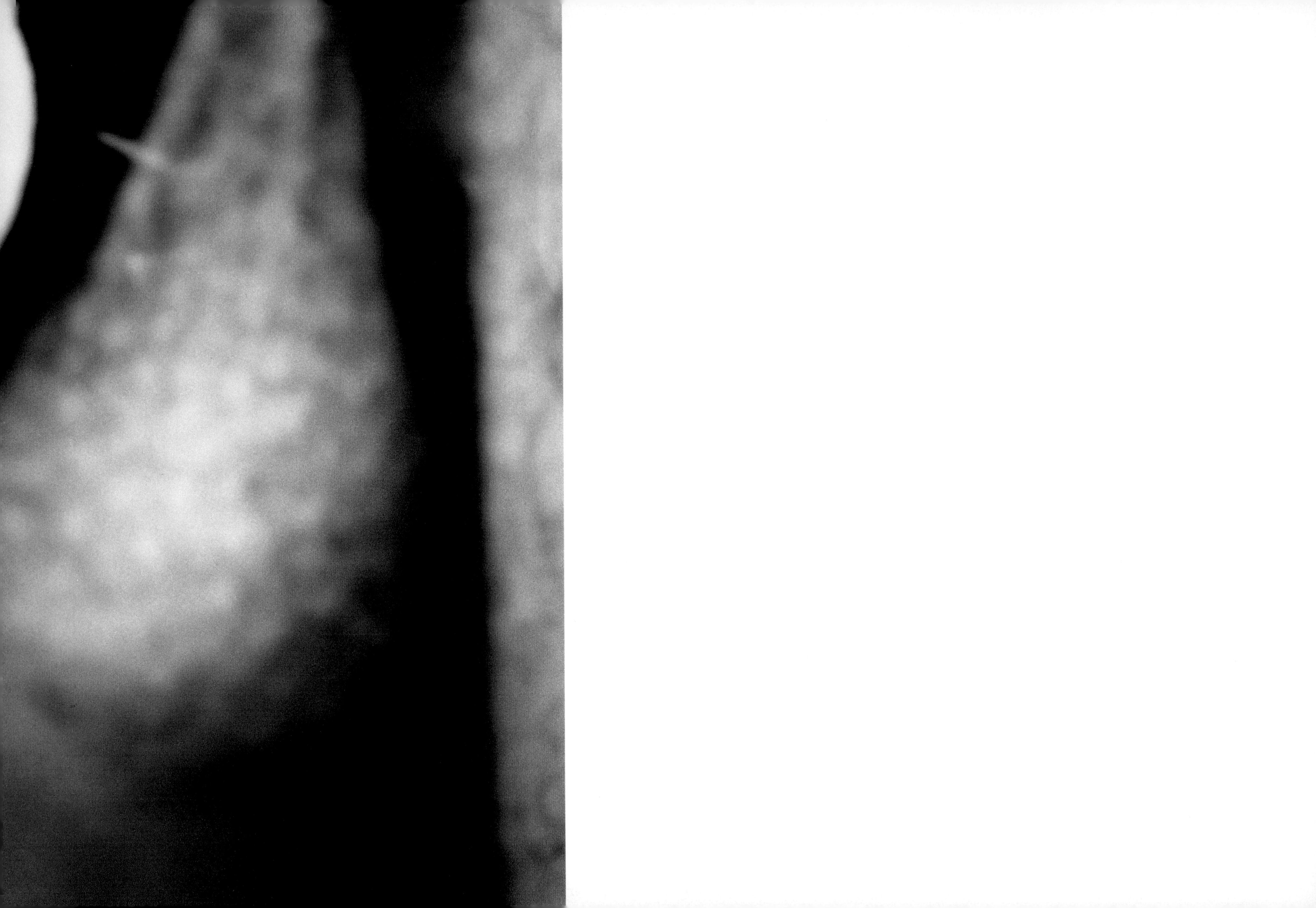

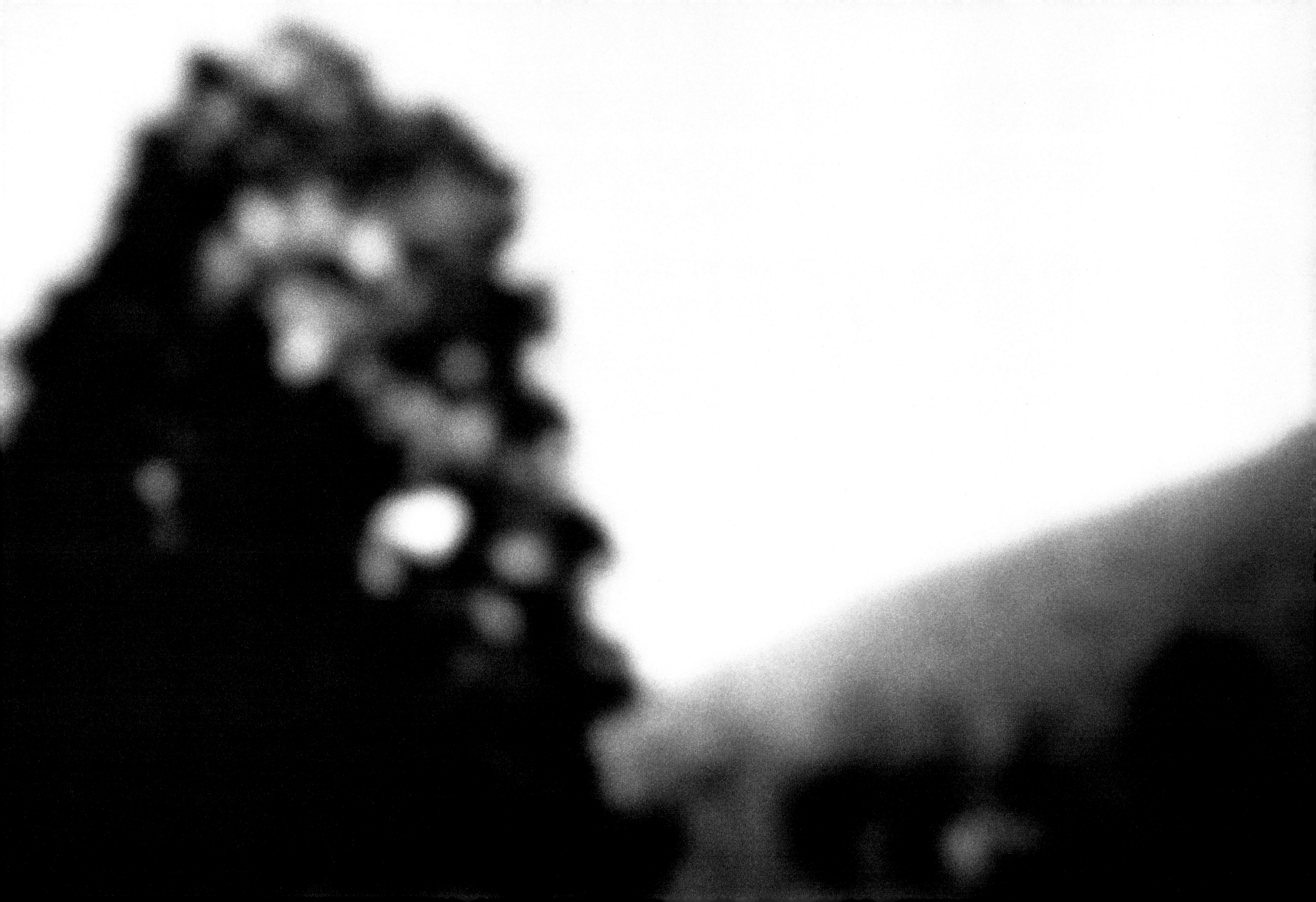

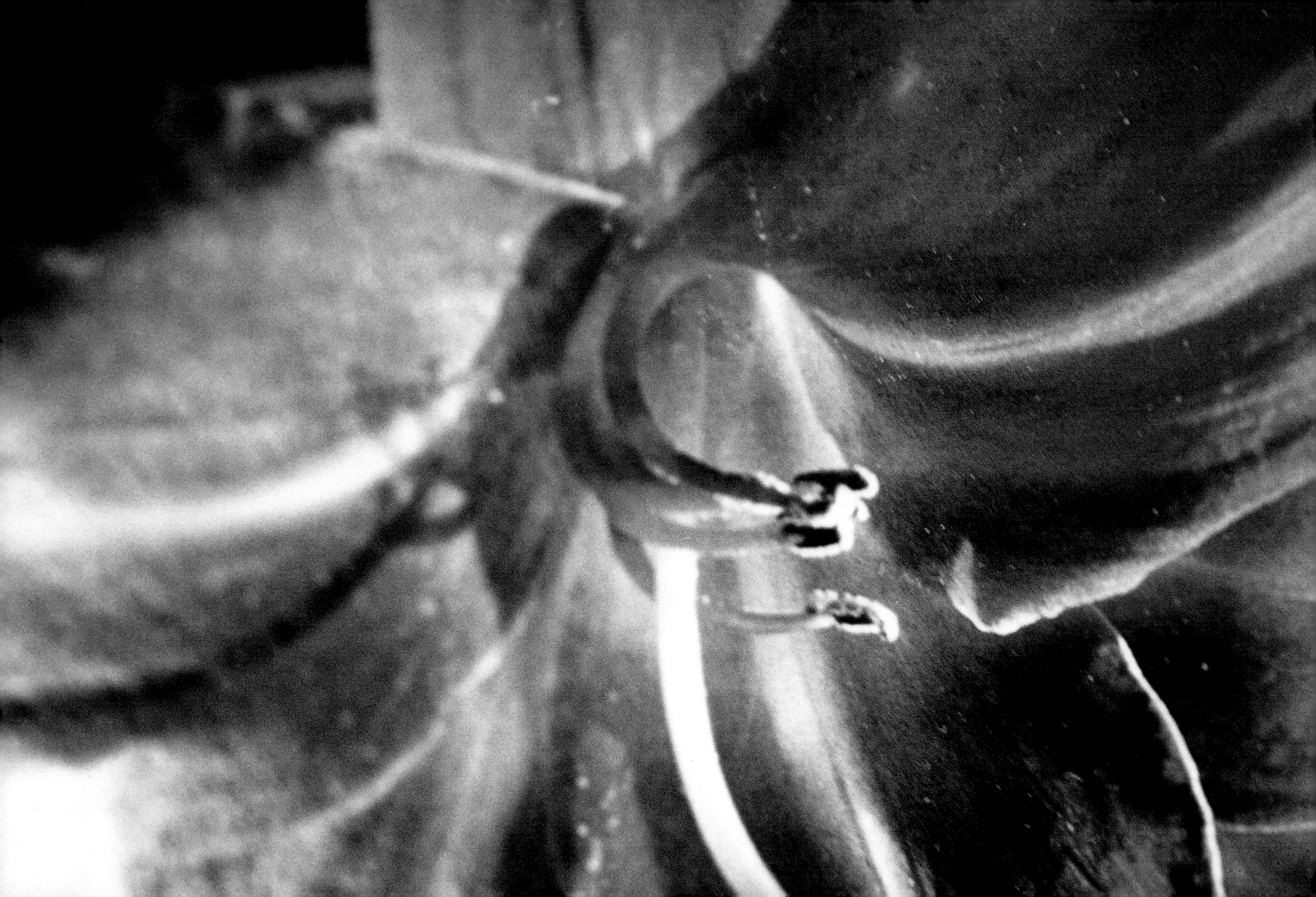

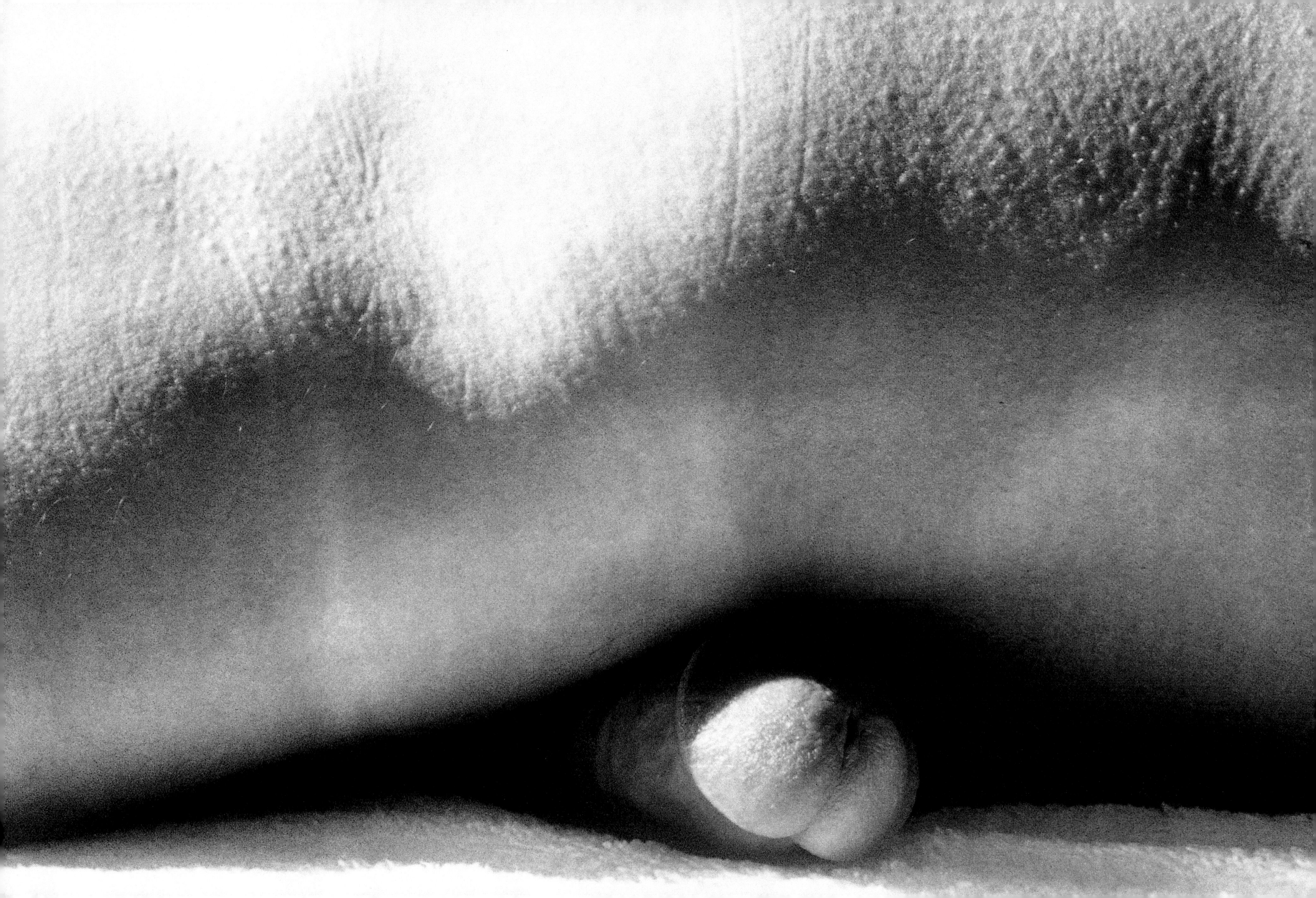

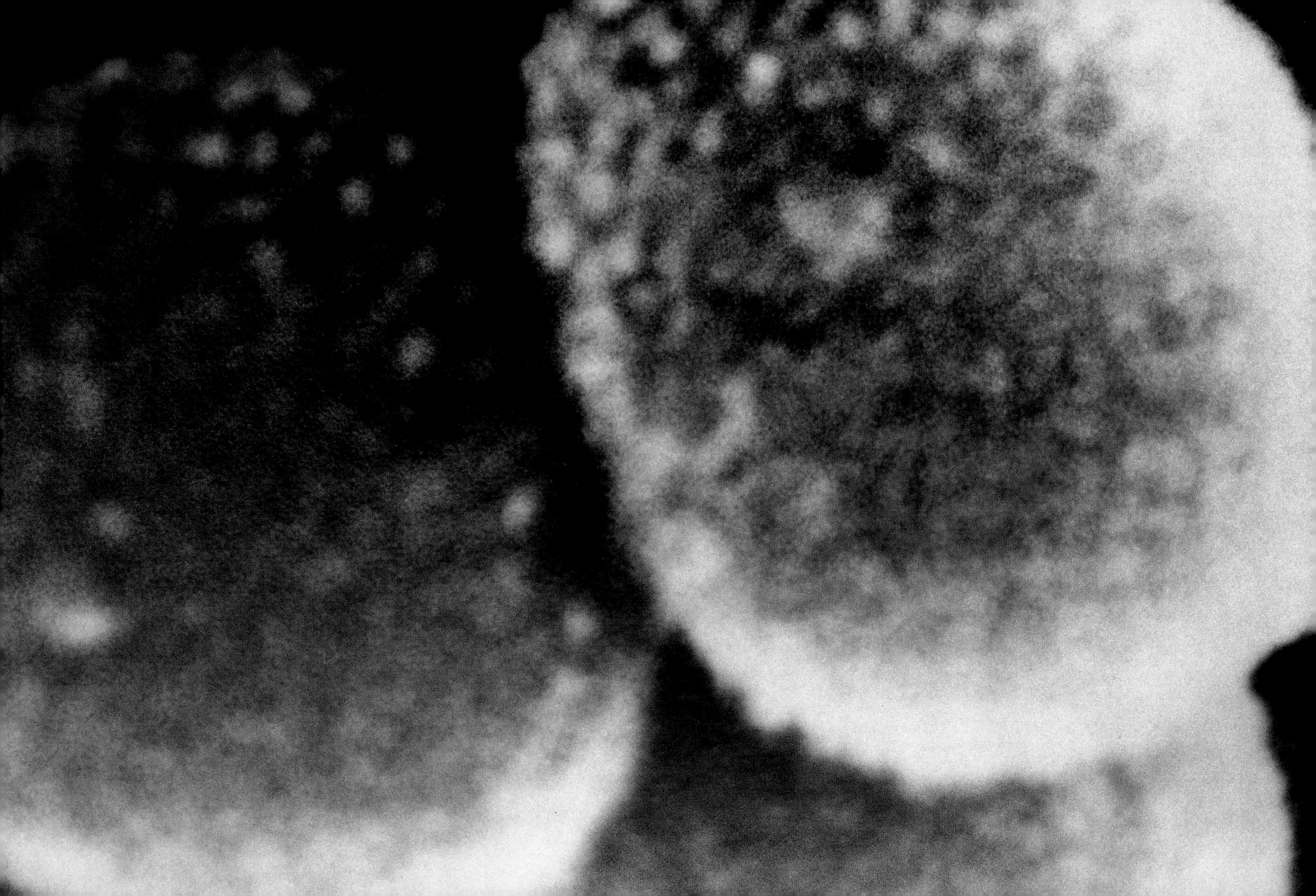

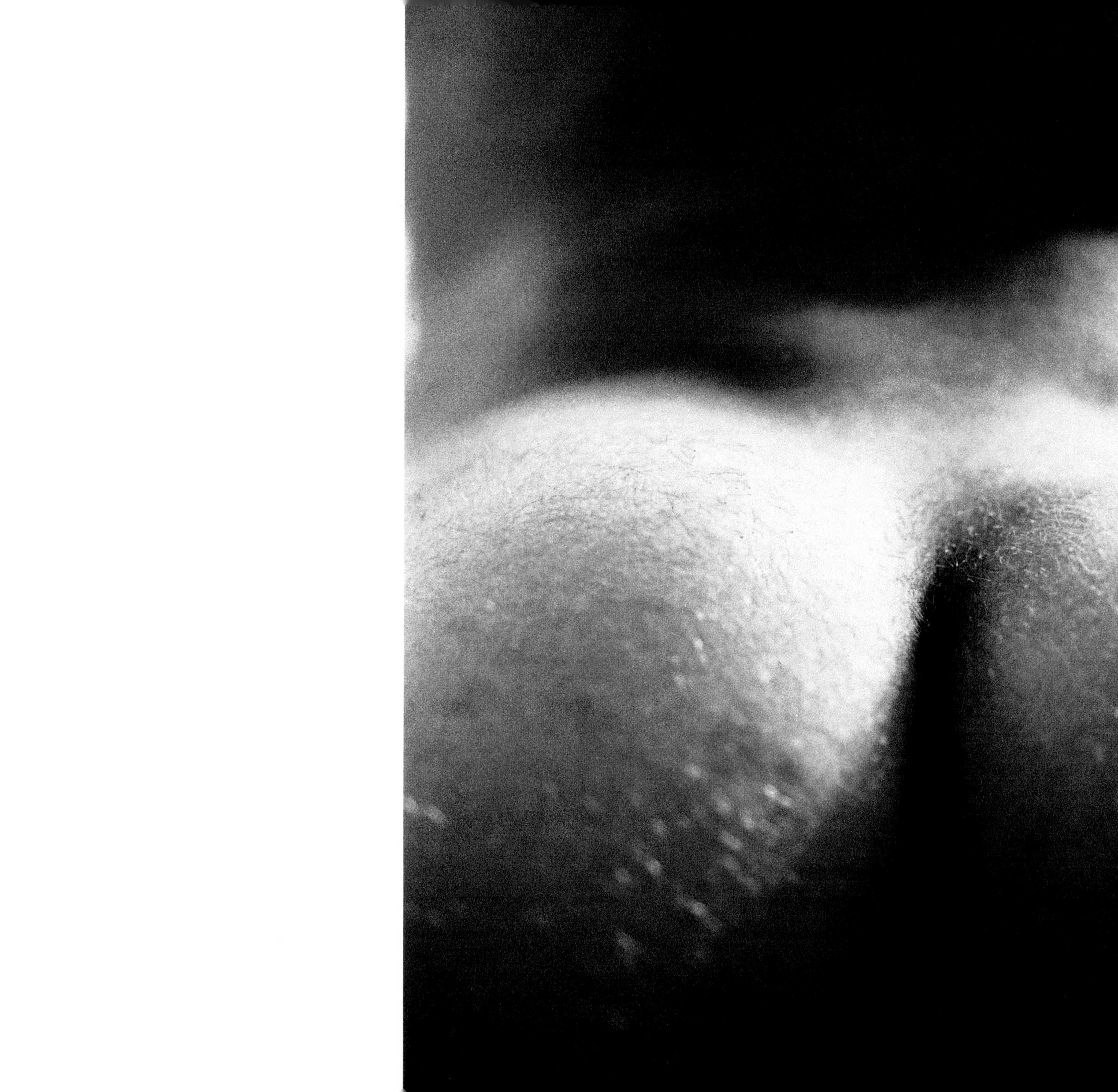

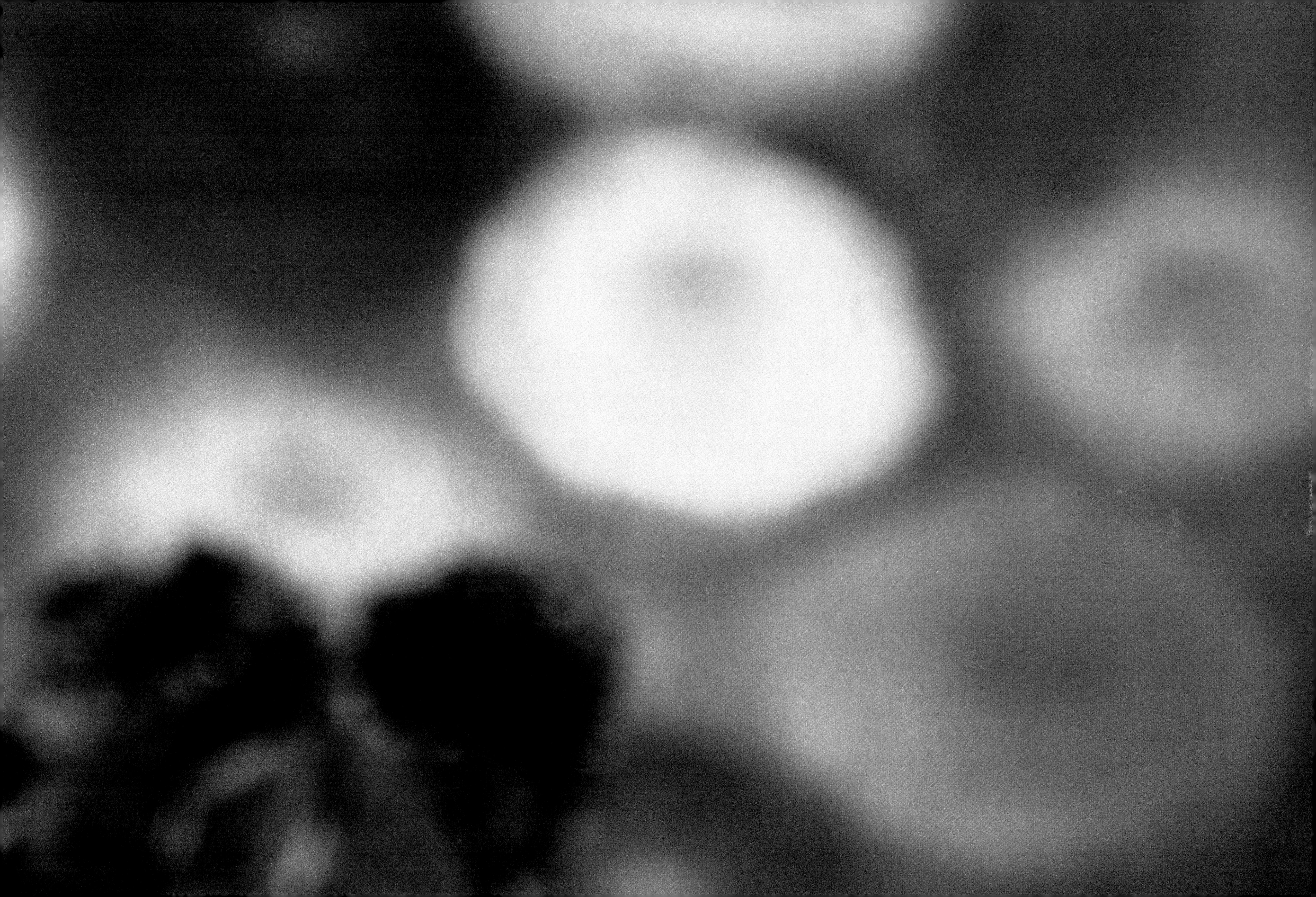

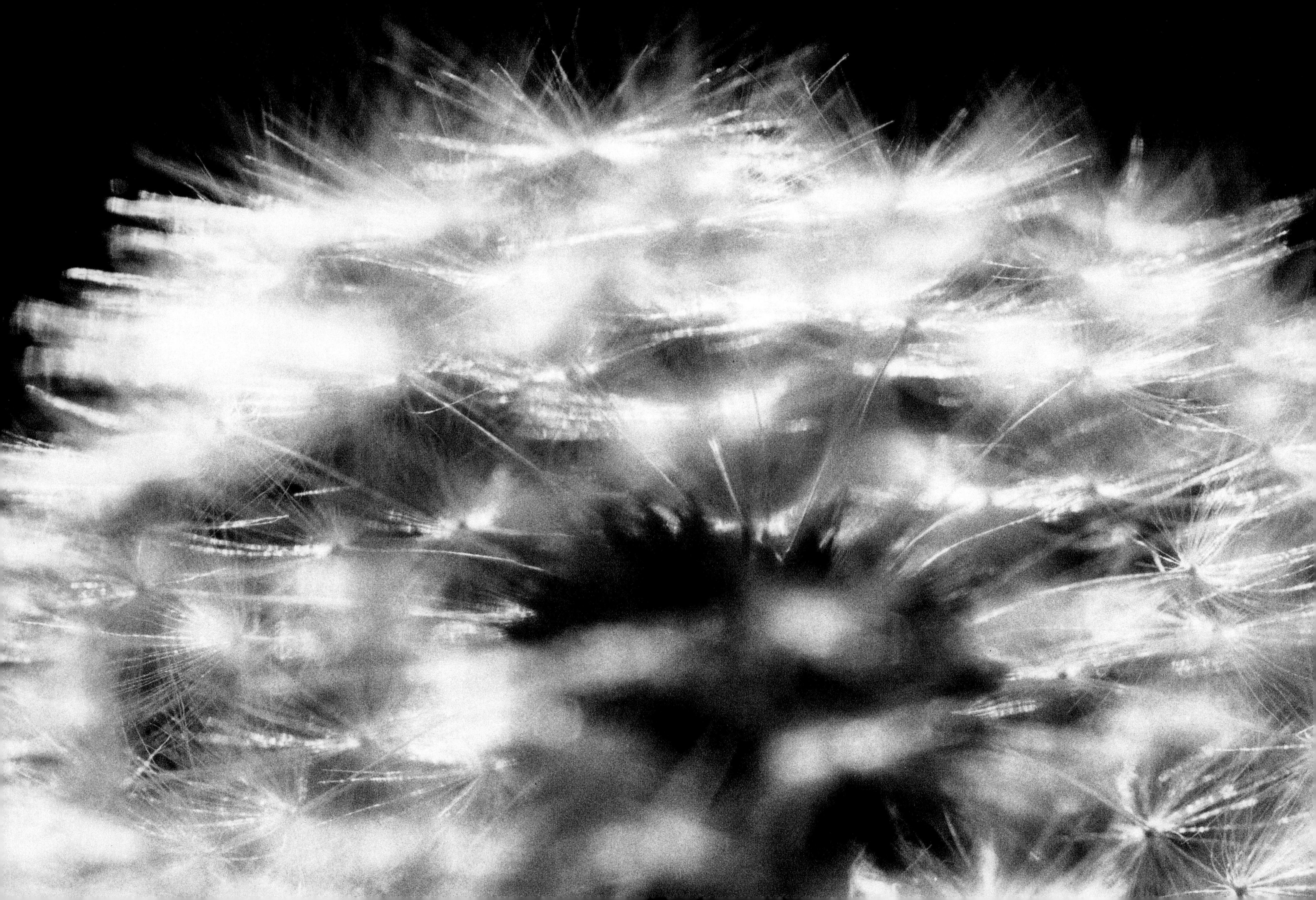

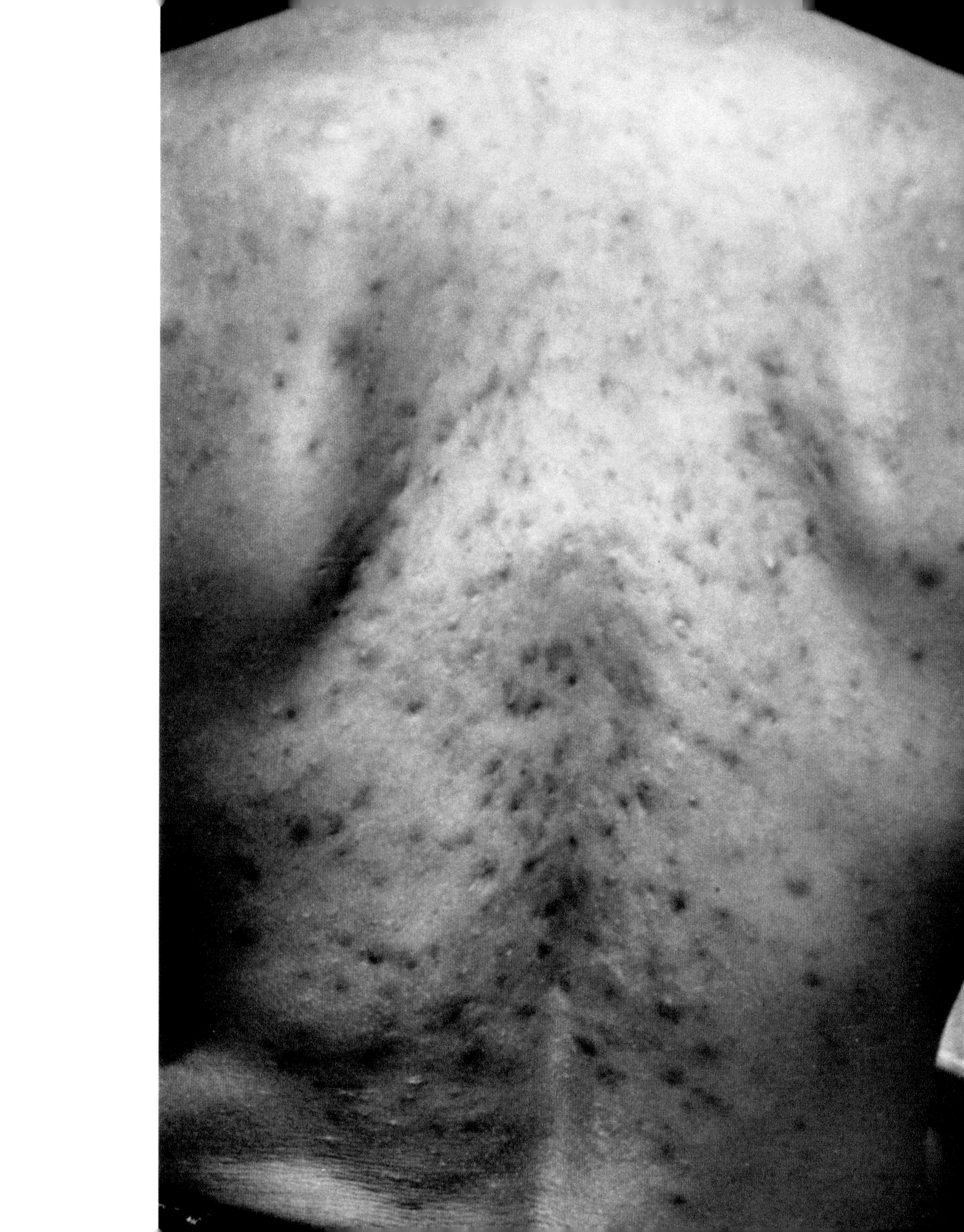

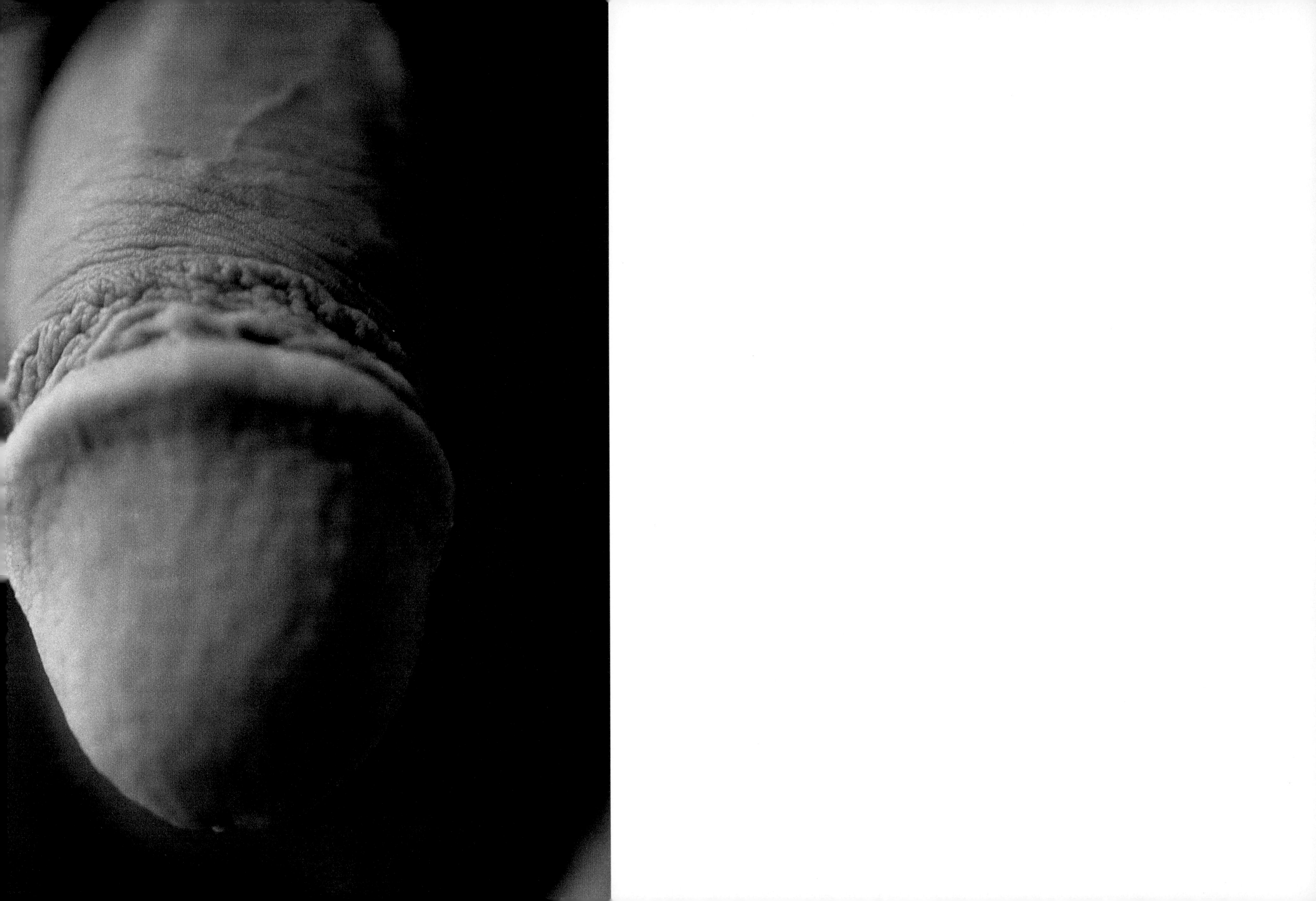

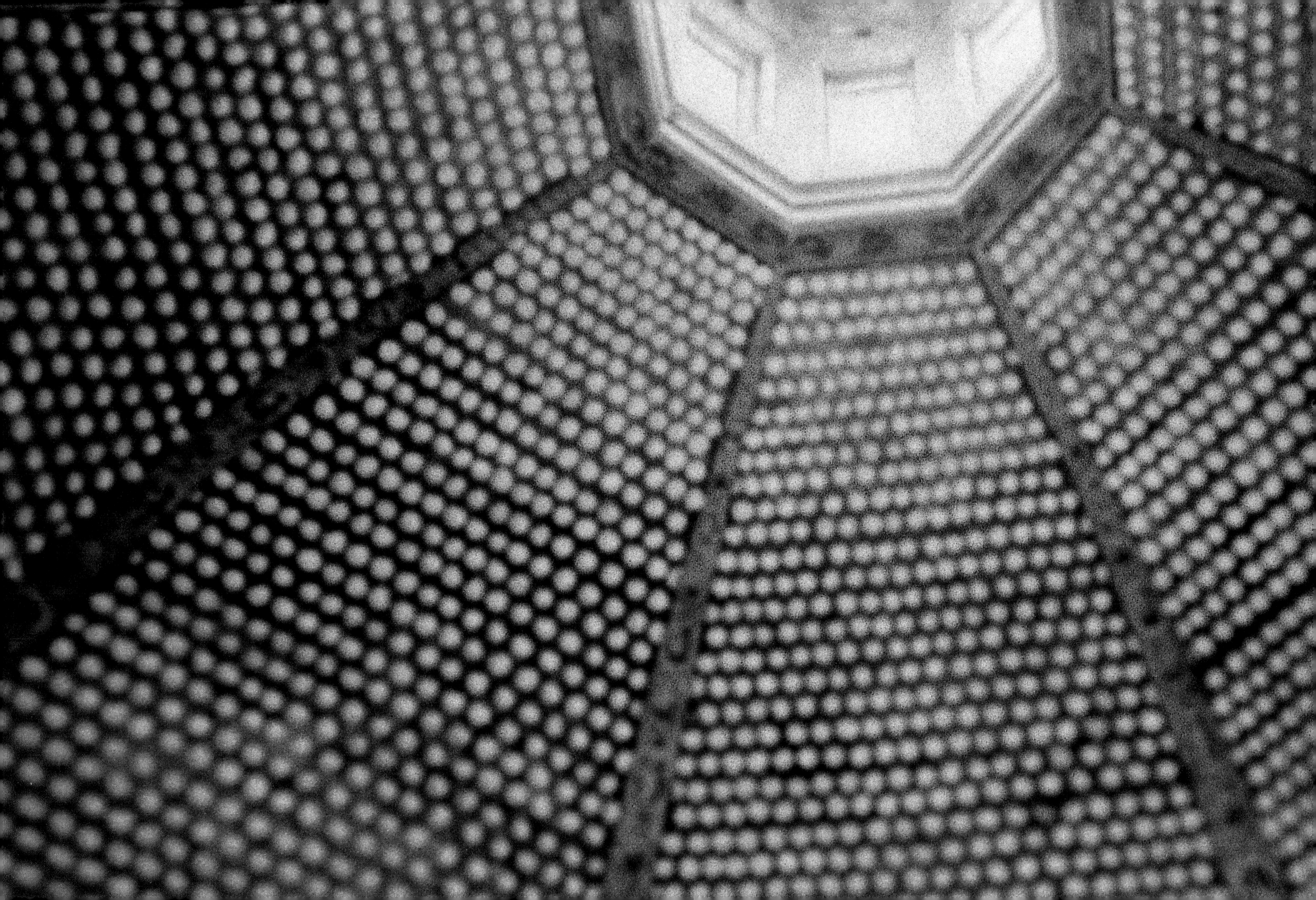

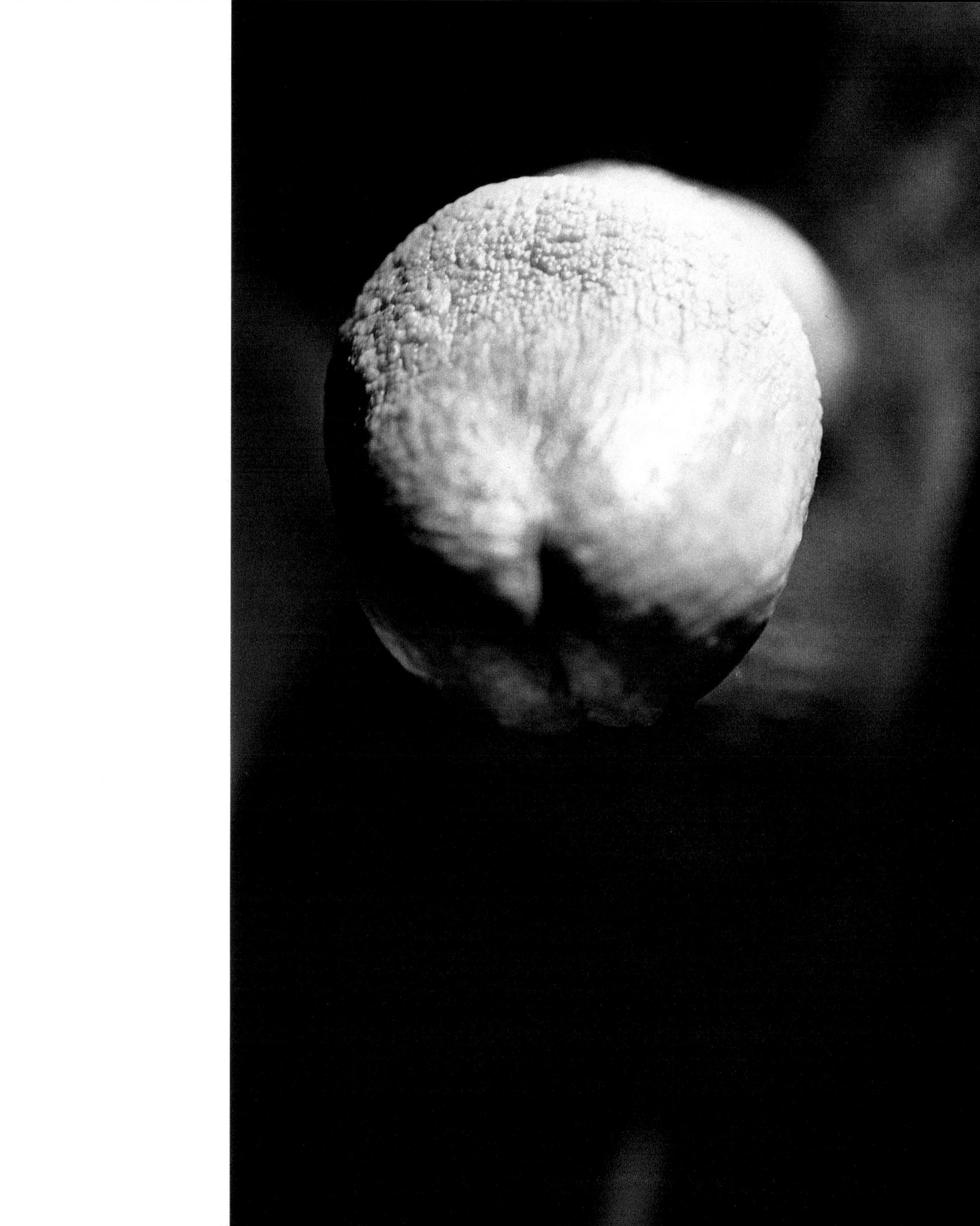

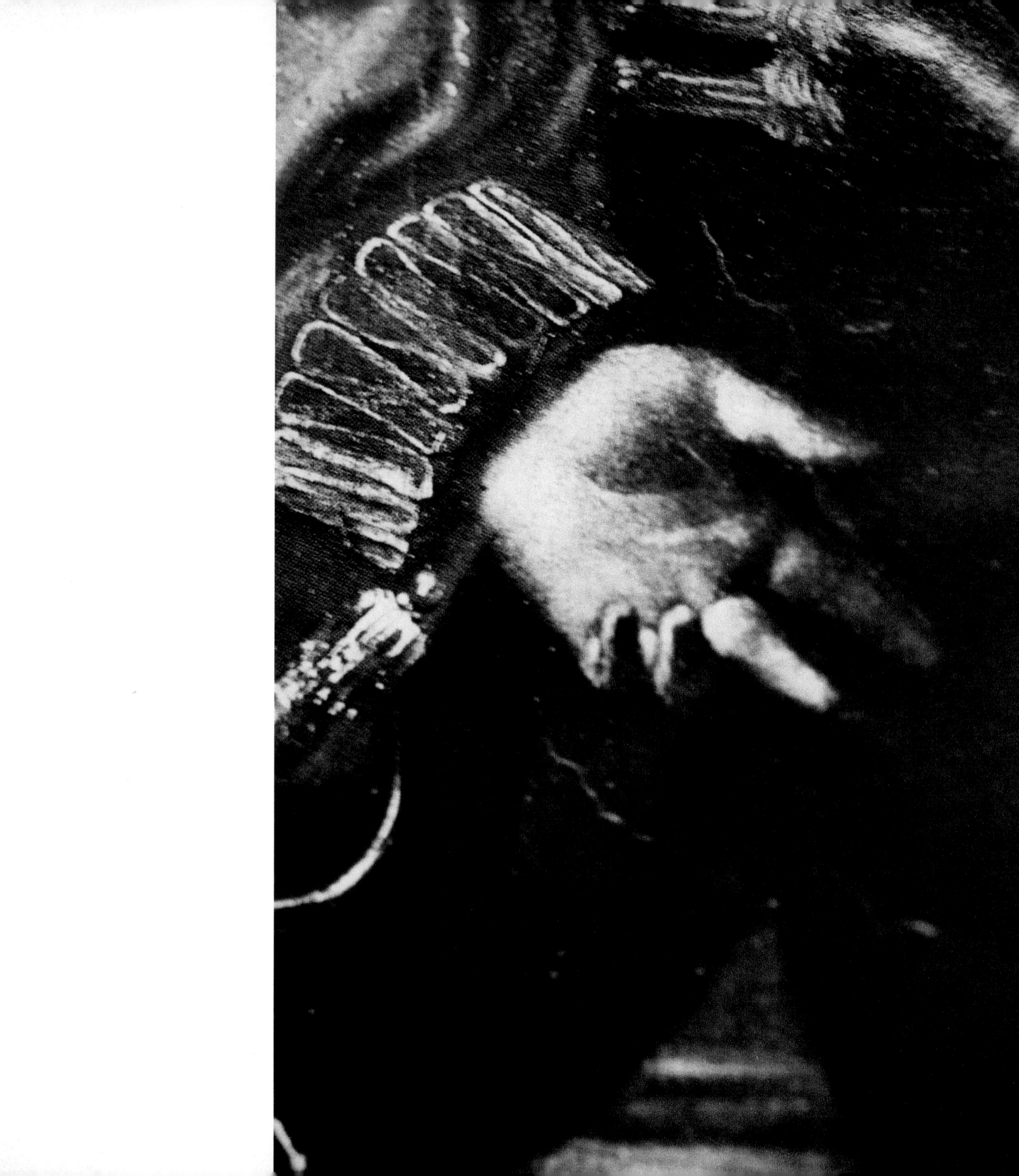

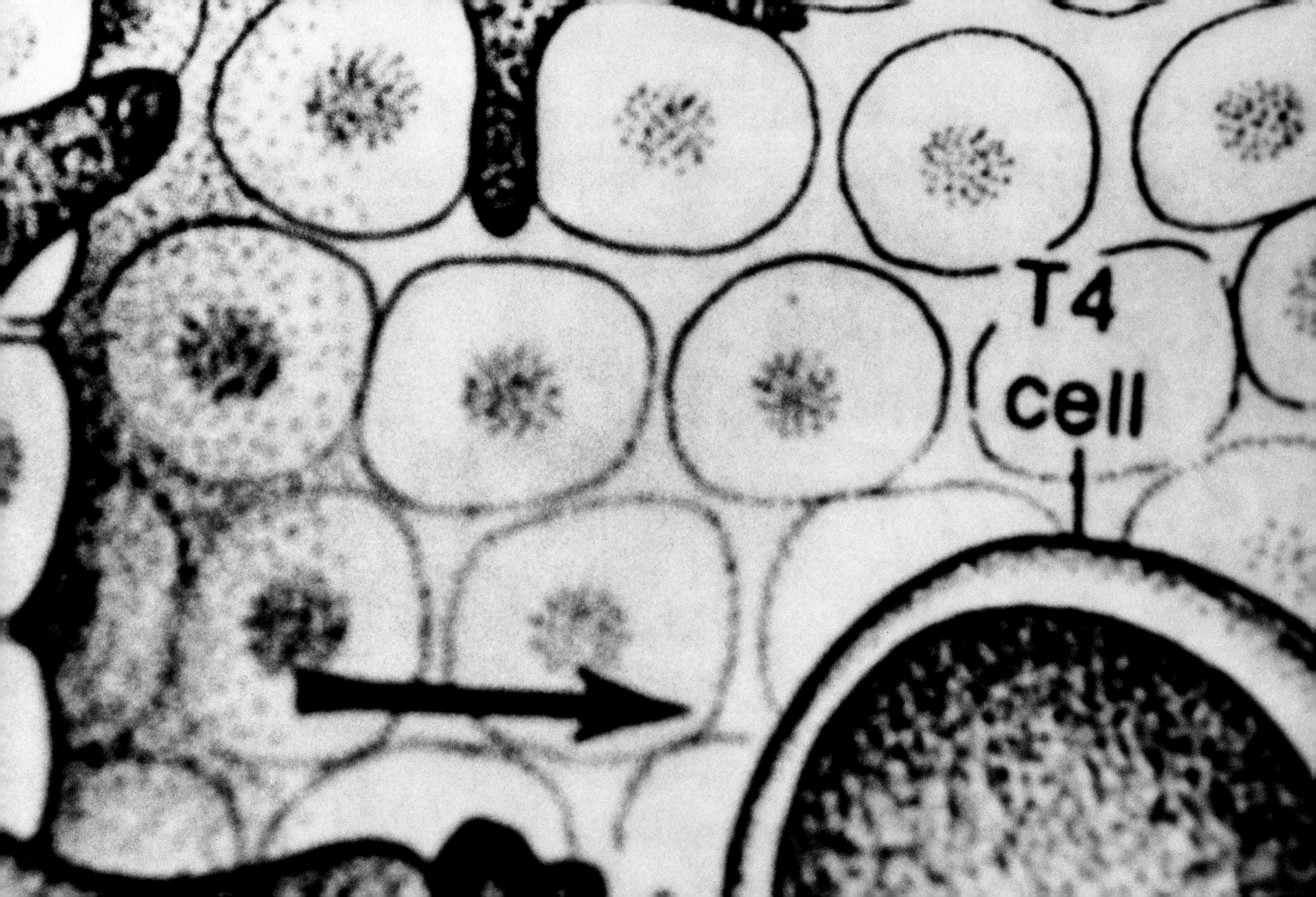

T4
Cell

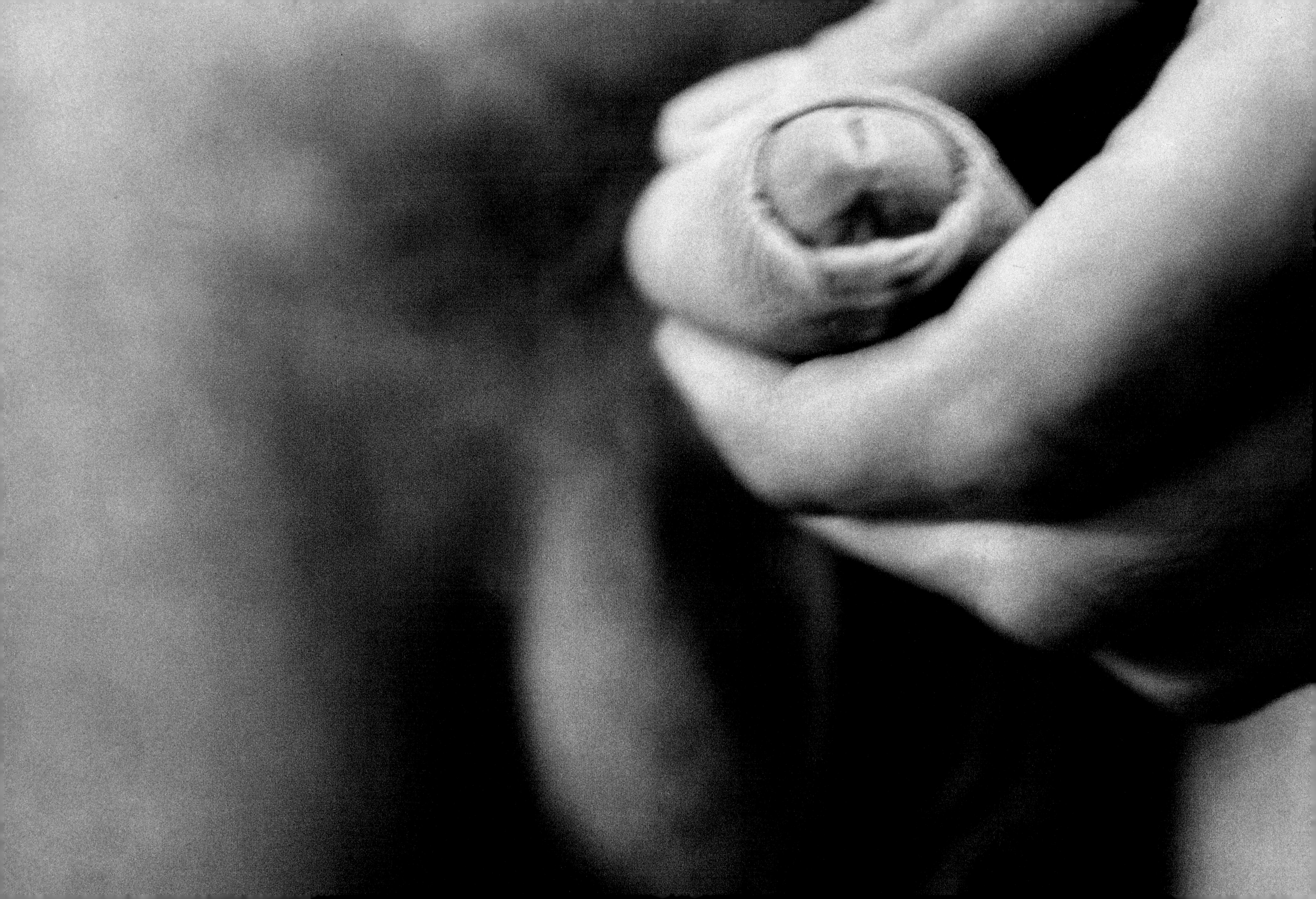

ity on behalf of man. When I looked at man, I did not see a piece of noble work, a species whose every member was automatically of infinite worth and the pinnacle of Nature's efforts. Nor did history, as I read it, support such grandiose claims. Throughout human time, men had been murdering men with an ease that suggested they took a profound pleasure in it."

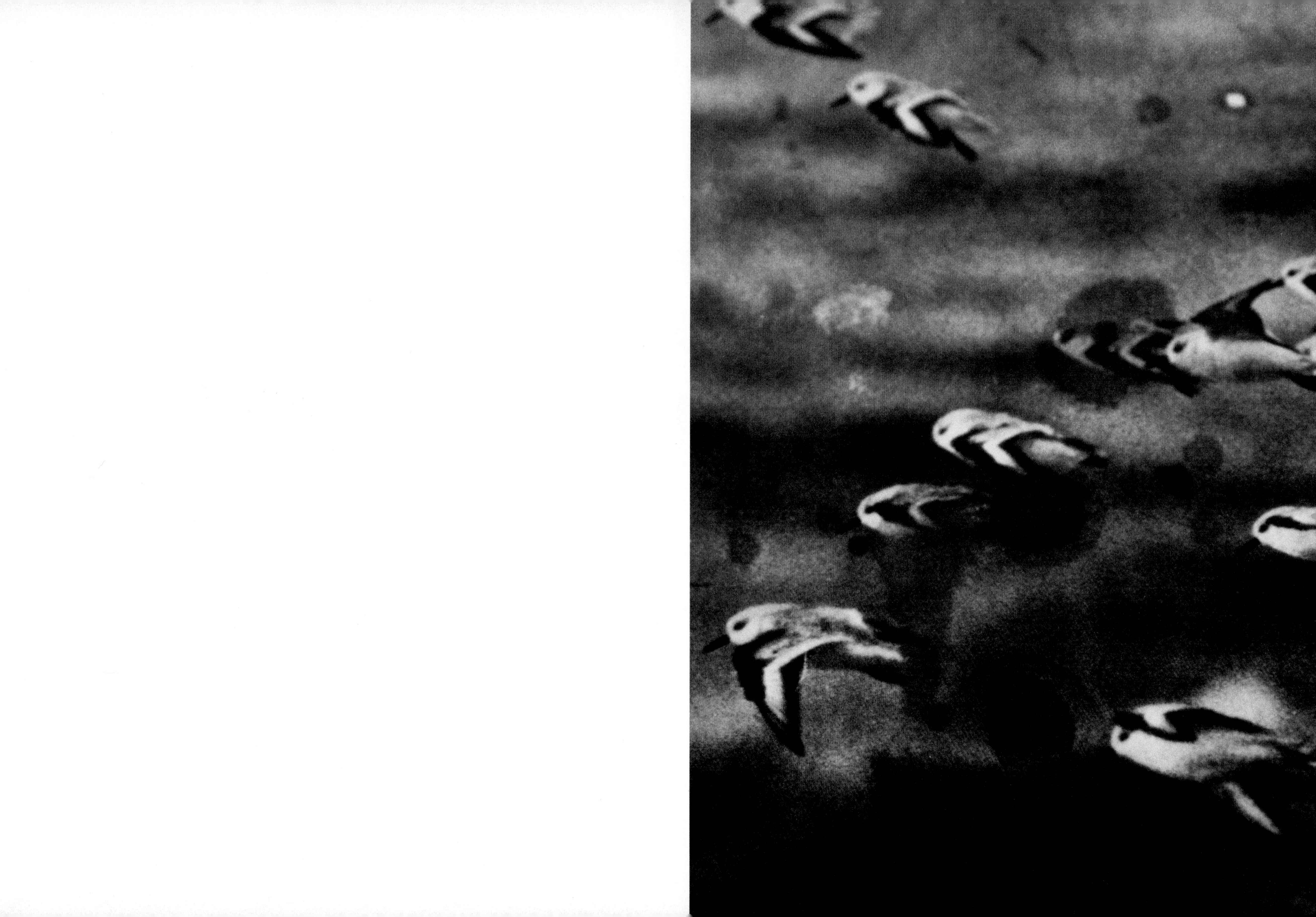

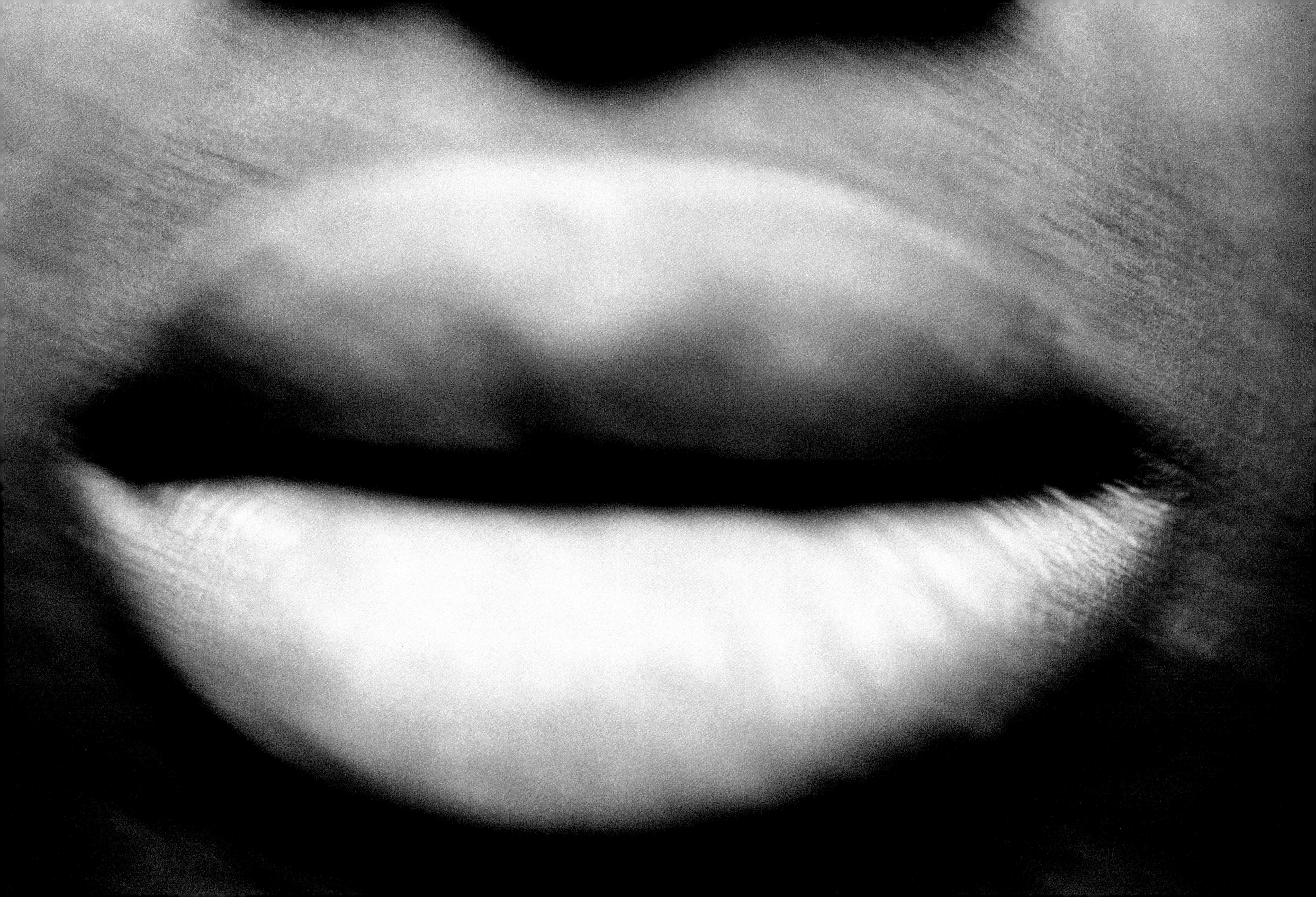

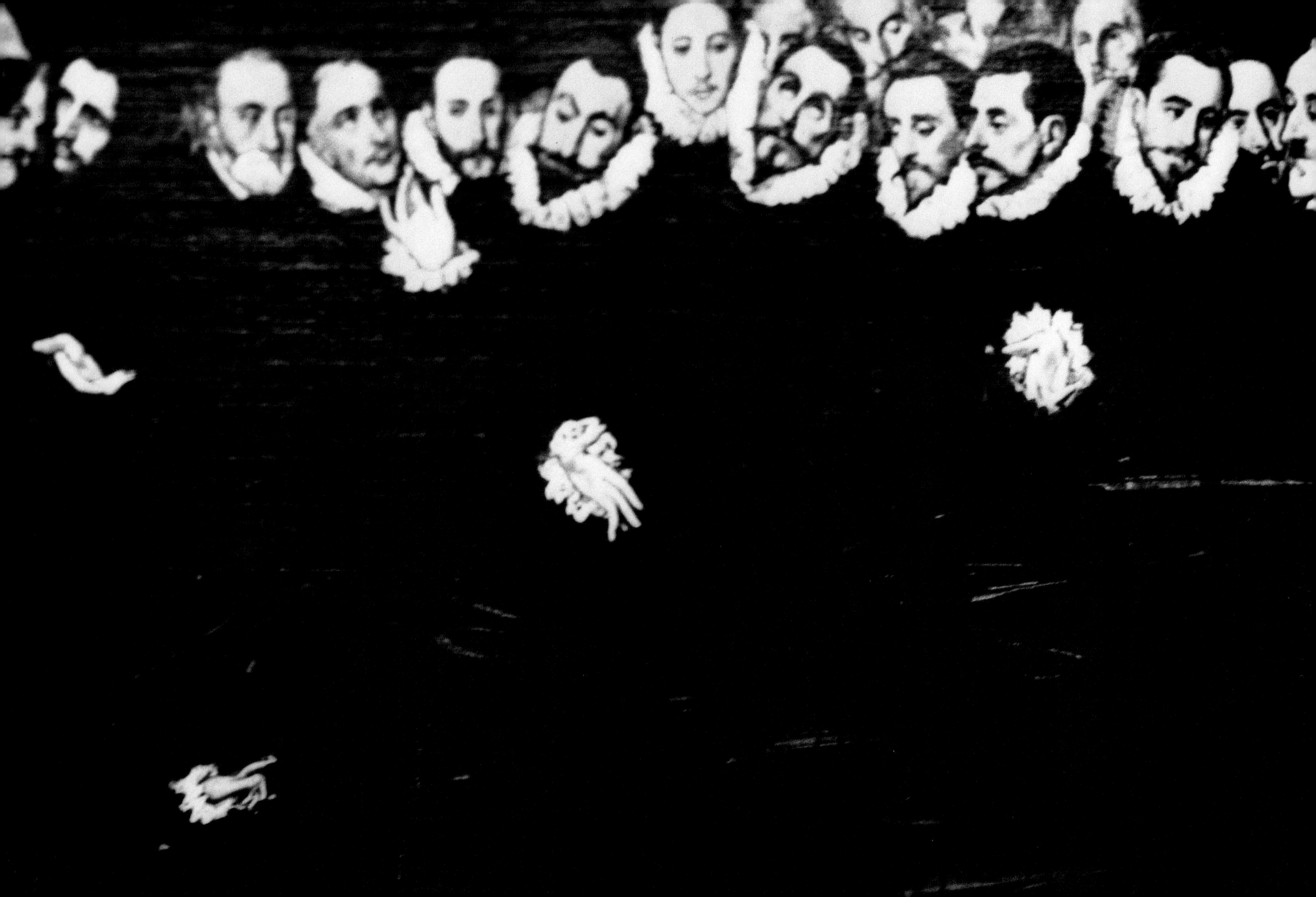

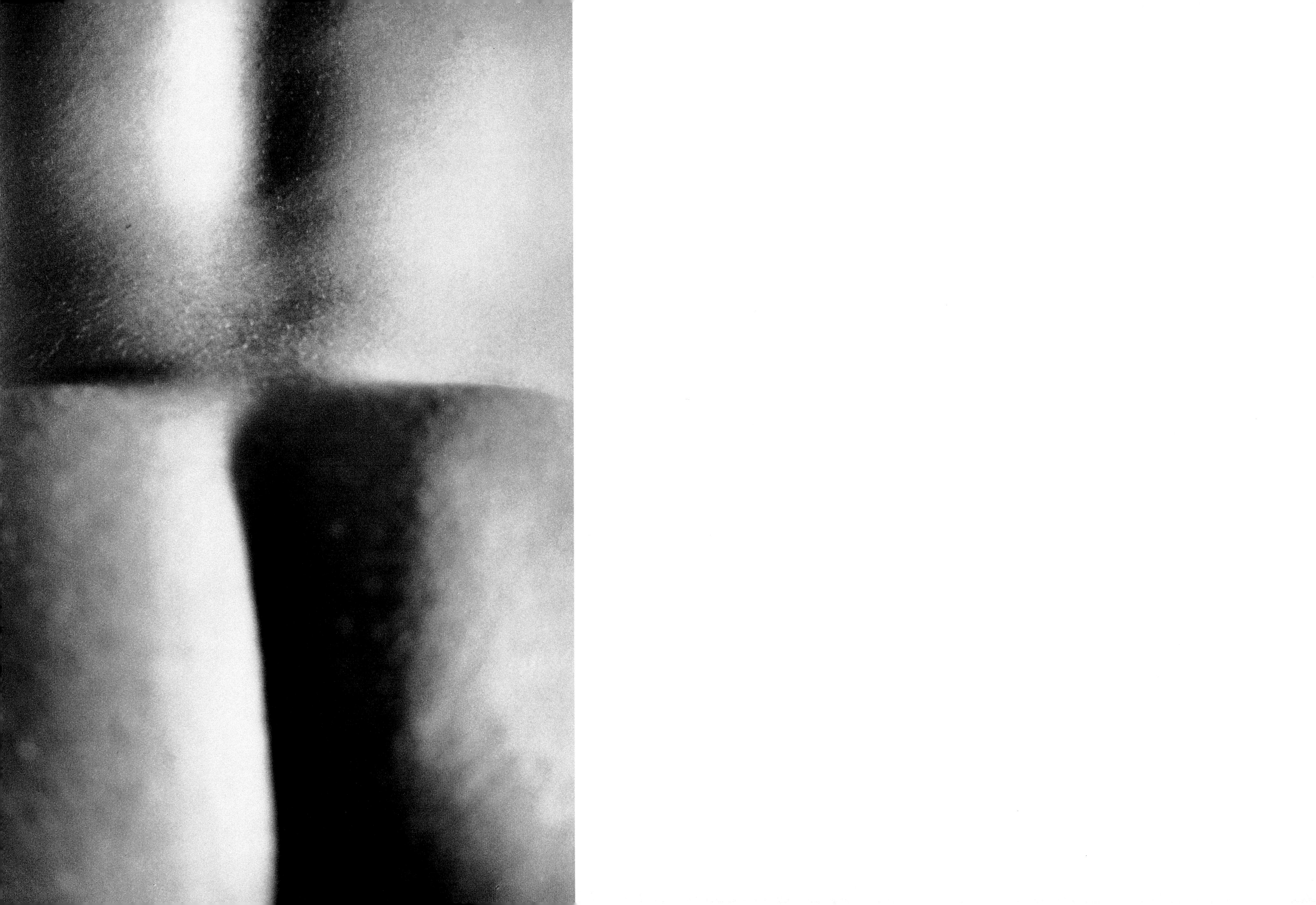

kind of exercise, he thinks. "It has to do with empathy, with our capacity as artists and as viewers to transfer our feelings. As a viewer, you've got to participate bodily when you look at a painting. A painting is a physical metaphor, an extension of nerves, muscles, gestures, and to grasp it you've got to feel yourself in it."

He smiles. "Picasso supposedly

"Railing against something doesn't mean you've escaped from it," he writes. "The grand theme of your career may be that the burden of representation is an illusion — a paradigm, par excellence, of ideological mauvaise foi — but that will only heighten your chagrin when you realize that it follows you everywhere like your own shadow. It isn't a thing of your making, and it won't succumb to your powers of unmaking —

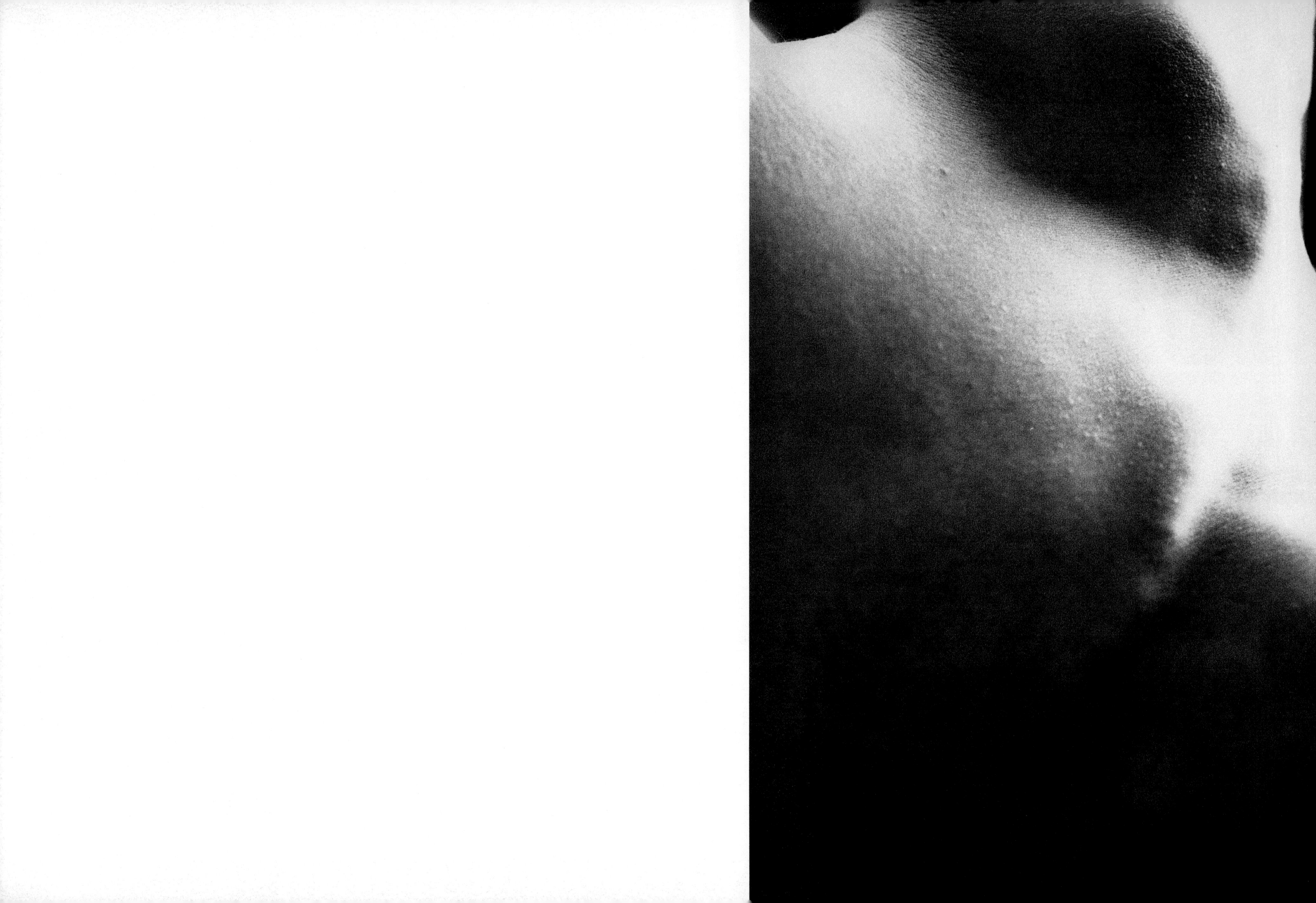

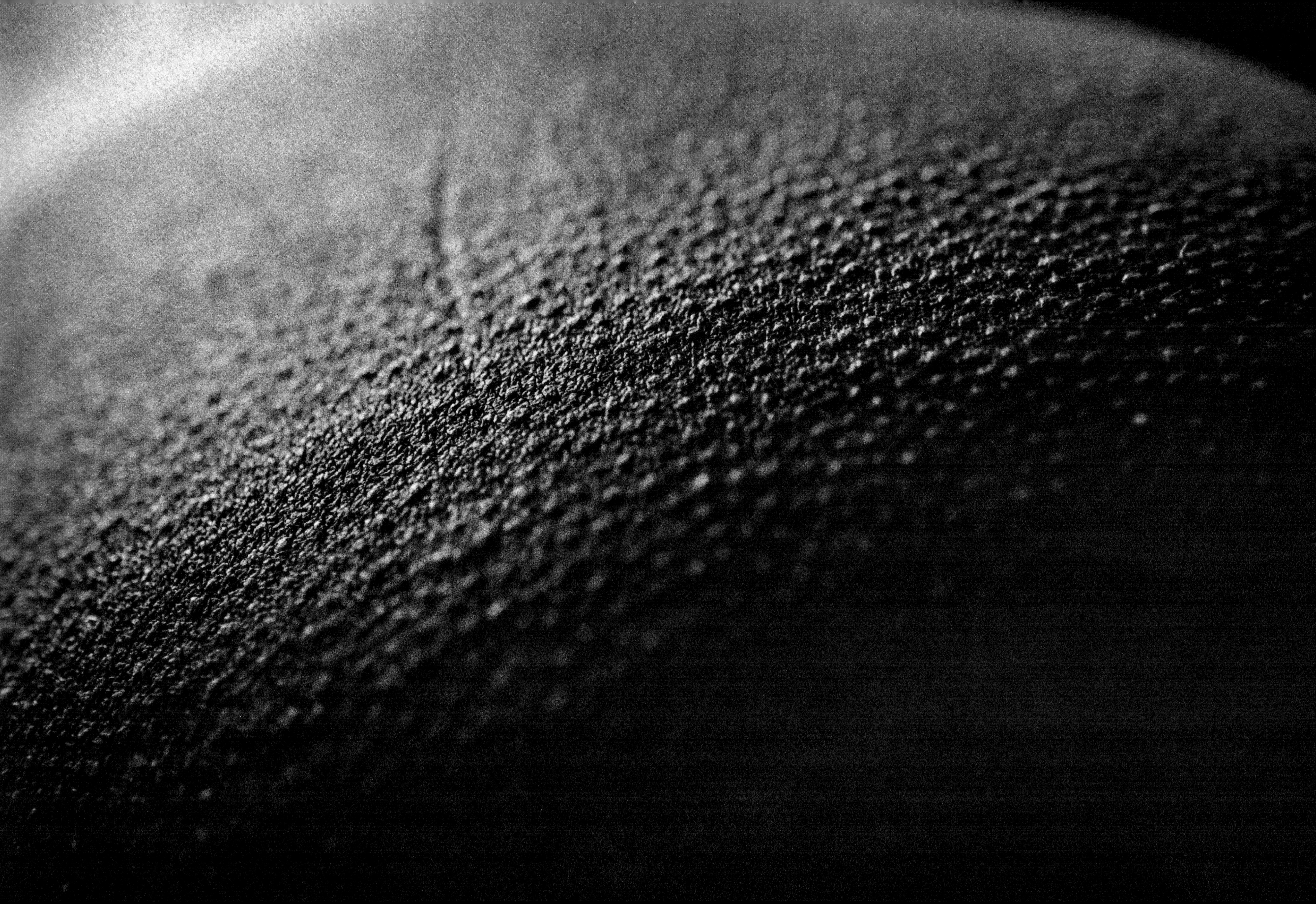

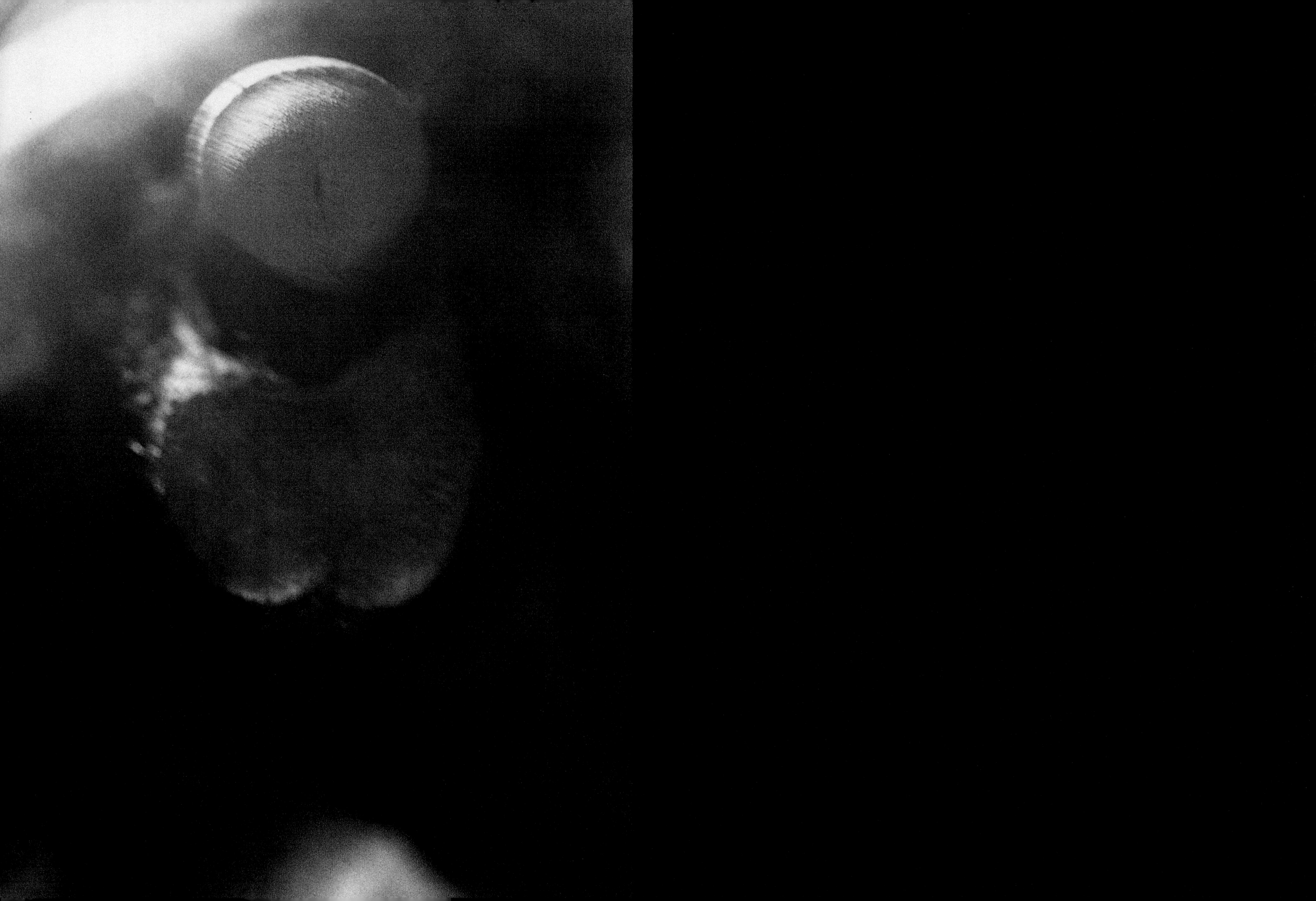

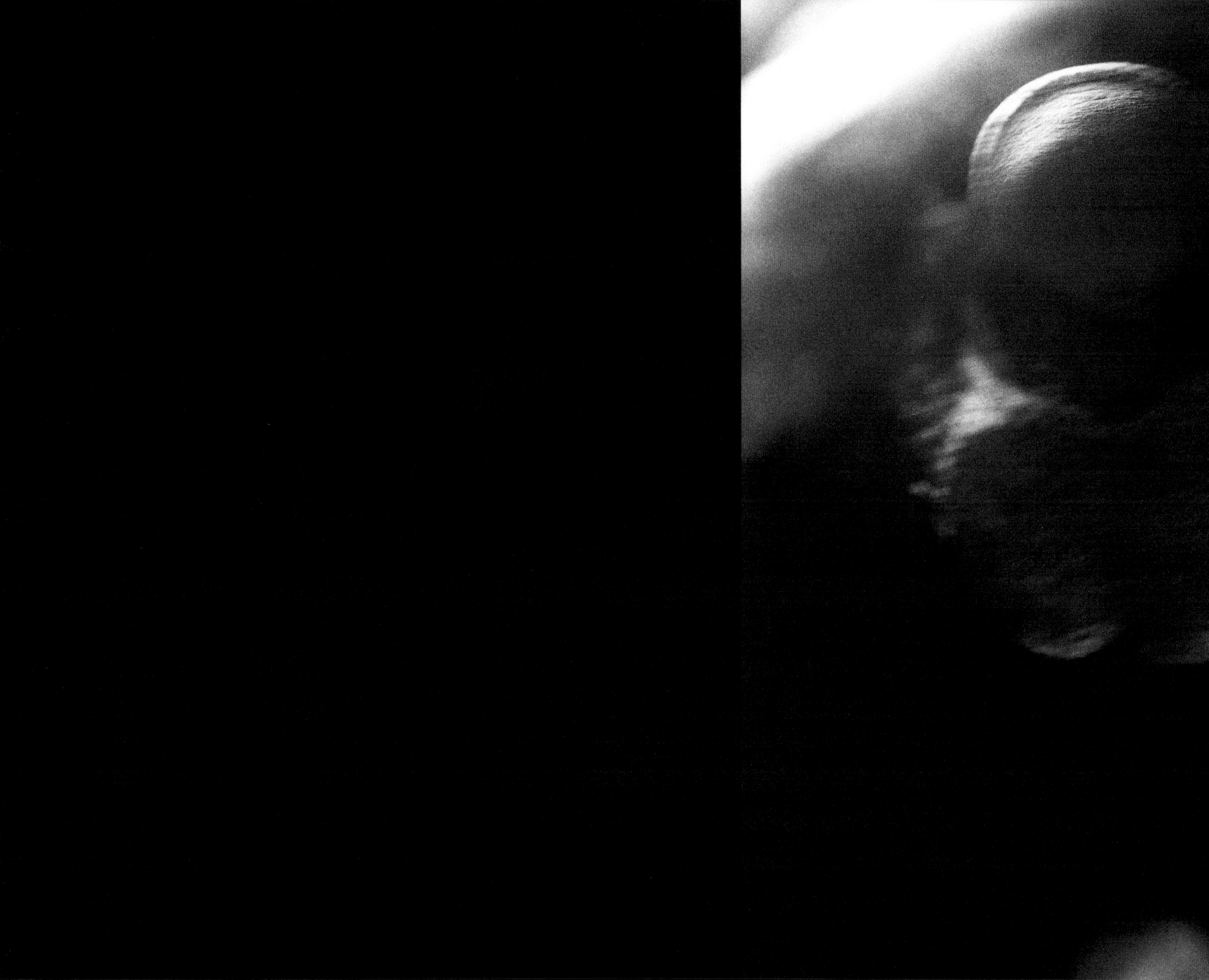

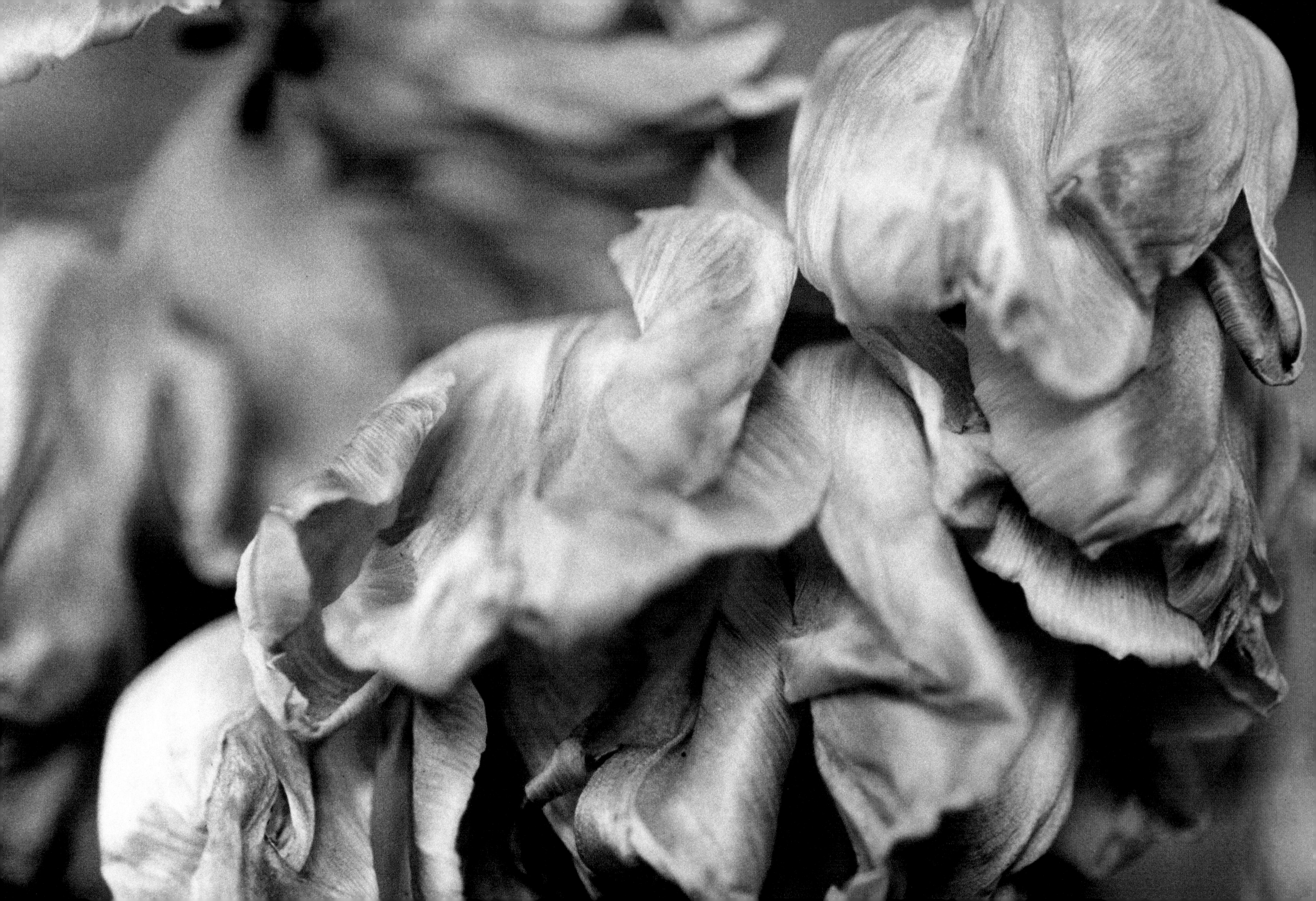

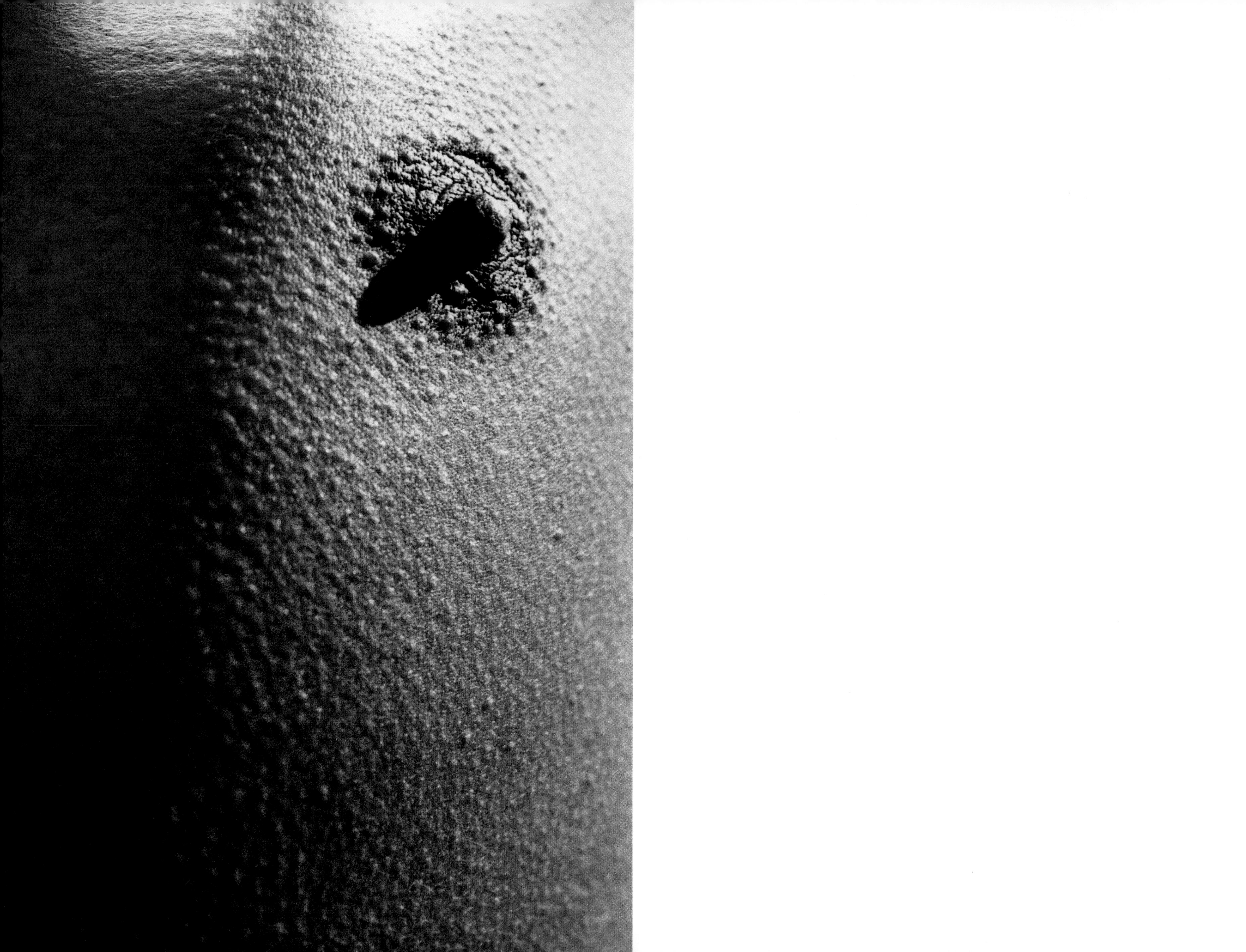

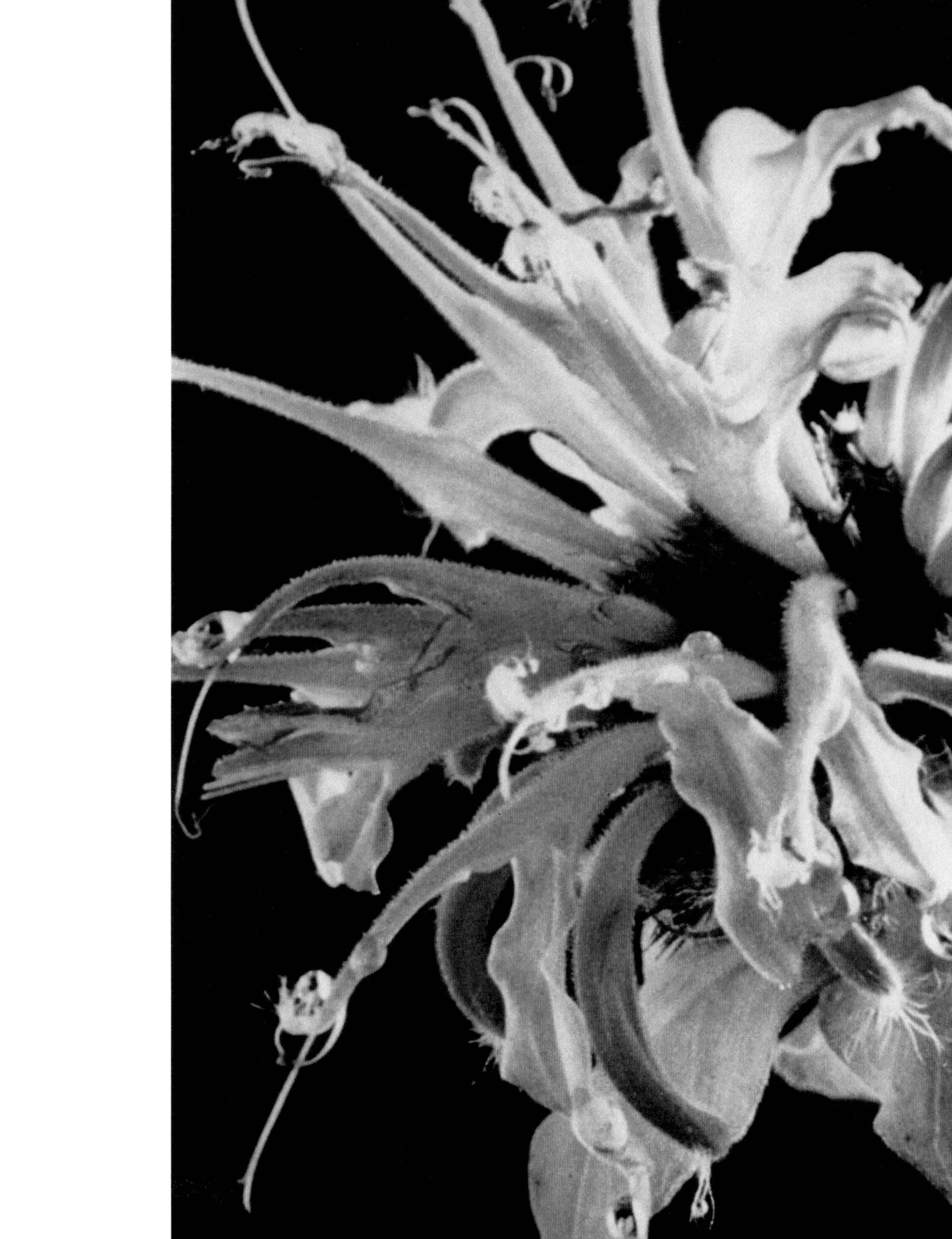

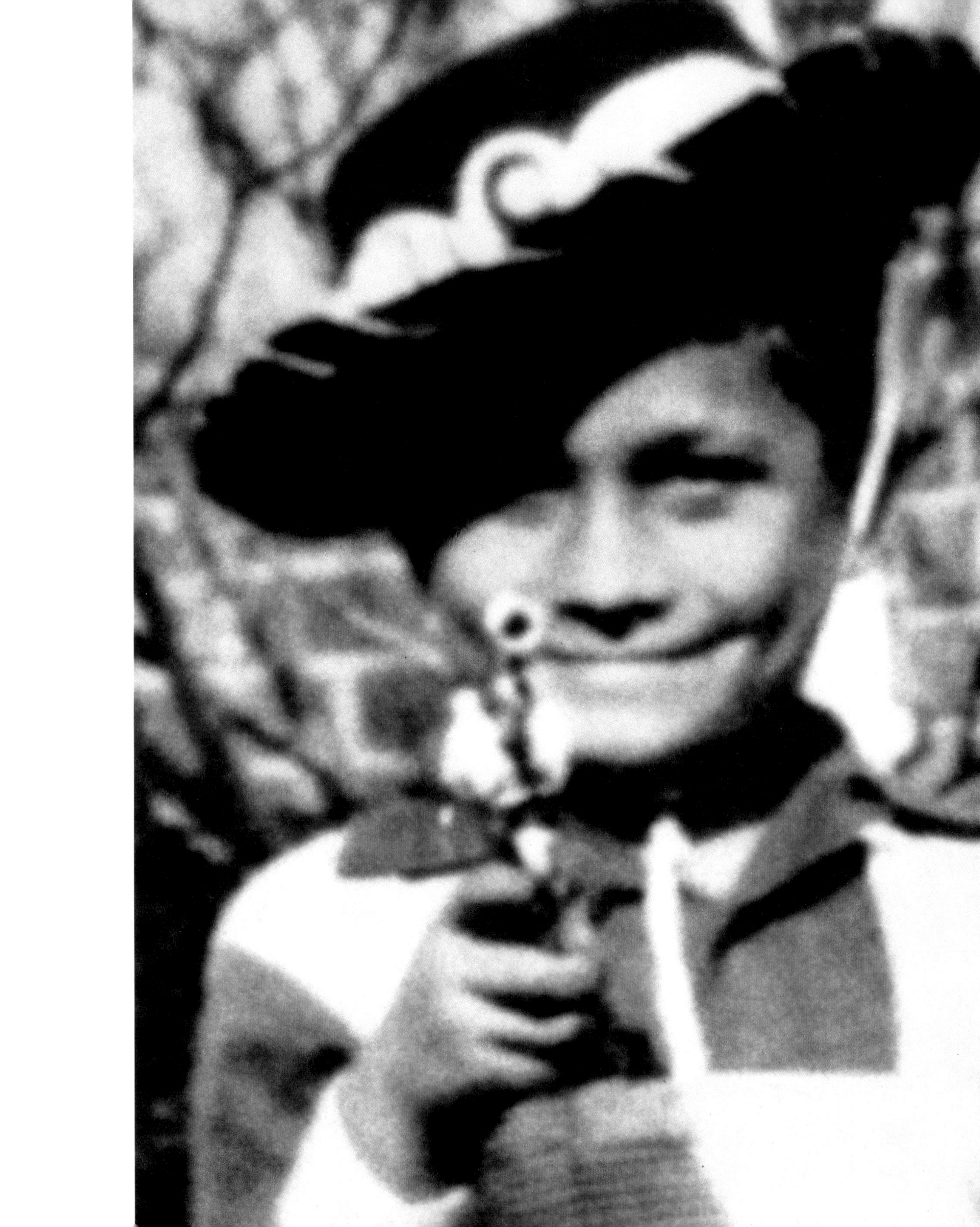

many years ago."

A Senator when he died, Mr. Ribeiro also reveled in his reputation as an incurable flirt. To celebrate his 73d birthday in November 1995, Mr. Ribeiro, who never had children, gathered the 50 women he loved most in his life. The only men at the party were the waiters.

To Mr. DaMatta Mr. Ribeiro was

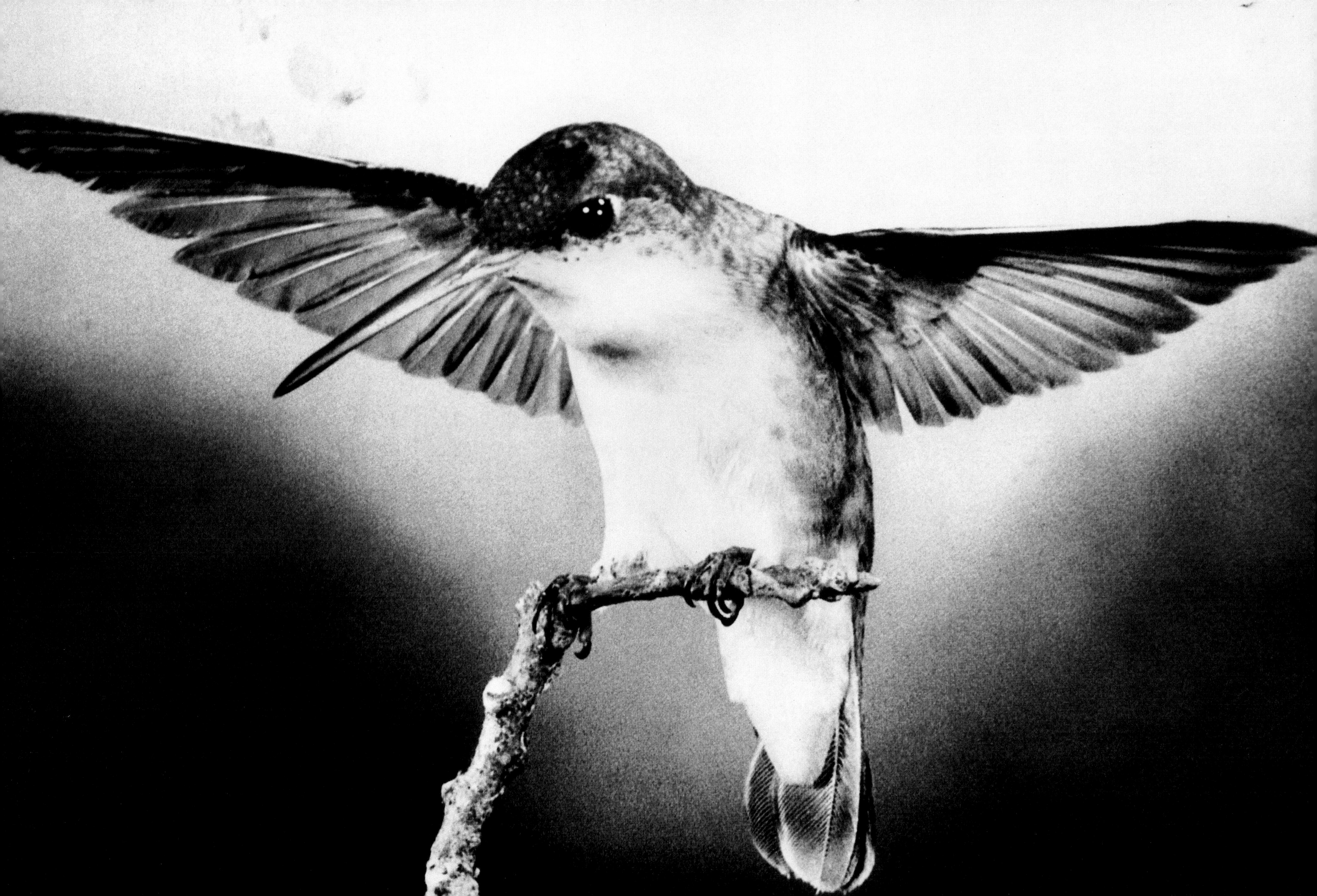

This first edition of Ross Bleckner, Page Three is limited to 3,000 casebound copies. A numbered edition of 100 copies in a clamshell box with an original watercolor by the artist accompanies the regular edition. The photographs are copyright Ross Bleckner 1998 and this edition is copyright Twin Palms Publishers 1998. Printed and bound in Japan for Twin Palms Publishers, post office box 10229, Santa Fe, New Mexico 87504. Regular edition : ISBN 0-944092-60-6. Limited edition : ISBN 0-944092-59-4.

Art direction and design by Tony Payne and Jack Woody.

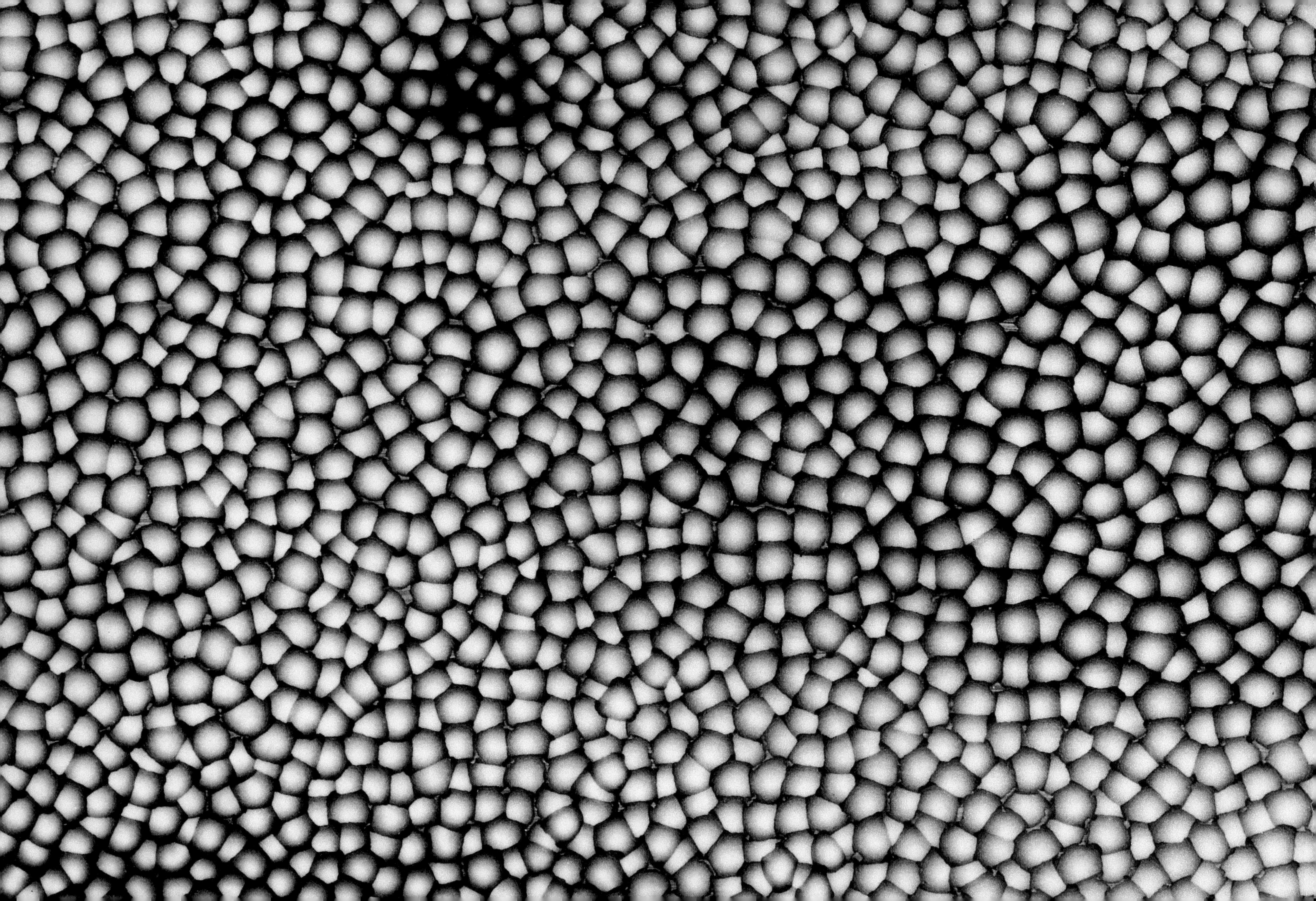